WORDS
TO LIVE BY

WORDS
TO LIVE BY

A MEMOIR BY

WILLIAM WHITEHEAD

Cormorant Books

**Canada Council
for the Arts** **Conseil des Arts
du Canada** 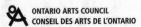 **ONTARIO ARTS COUNCIL
CONSEIL DES ARTS DE L'ONTARIO**

Canadian Patrimoine
Heritage canadien   Canadä

The publisher gratefully acknowledges the support of the Canada Council for
the Arts and the Ontario Arts Council for its publishing program. We acknowledge
the financial support of the Government of Canada through the Canada Book Fund
(CBF) for our publishing activities, and the Government of Ontario through the
Ontario Media Development Corporation, an agency of the Ontario Ministry of
Culture, and the Ontario Book Publishing Tax Credit Program.

Library and Archives Canada Cataloguing in Publication

Whitehead, William, 1931–
Words to live by : a memoir / William Whitehead.

Issued also in electronic formats.
ISBN 978-1-77086-202-9

1. Whitehead, William, 1931–. 2. Television producers and directors—
Canada—Biography. 3. Canadian Broadcasting Corporation--Employees—
Biography. 4. Authors, Canadian (English)—20th century—Biography. I. Title.

PN1992.4.W45A3 2012   791.45092   C2012-903492-4

Cover photograph and design: Angel Guerra/Archetype
Interior text design: Tannice Goddard, Soul Oasis Networking
Printer: Trigraphik LBF

Printed and bound in Canada.

The interior of this book is printed on 100% post-consumer waste recycled paper.

Cormorant Books Inc.
390 Steelcase Road East, Markham, Ontario, L3R 1G2
www.cormorantbooks.com

This book is dedicated to the memory of Timothy Findley (Tiff),
who illuminated half my life —
And to Trevor Greene (Pooch),
who is superbly seeing me the rest of the way.

*Words are, of course, the most
powerful drug used by mankind.*

RUDYARD KIPLING
SPEECH, LONDON, 1923

Simpler Times

So — who the hell is William Whitehead? You probably know who Timothy Findley was — an internationally renowned writer known to friends and family by the initials of his full name: Timothy Irving Frederick Findley — Tiff. And if you ever attended one of his public appearances — a reading, a talk, a book signing — you may have noticed someone hovering nearby: someone tall, with a big smile, brown hair and eyes, carrying a bit too much weight and wearing a pen on a cord around his neck.

That was me.

(And now, some years after my companion's death, I still do double takes at headlines trumpeting the successes of the Toronto International Film Festival, whose acronym I find startling: TIFF.)

In our forty years together, I missed only one of Tiff's events. While he was giving an anti-censorship talk to a large gathering of librarians on the University of Toronto campus, I was locked away in the sound booth of a nearby film studio, recording one of the more than one hundred documentary narrations I had written.

When Tiff was done, he walked down to join me, still startled and a bit appalled to have discovered that most of the librarians seemed to be in favour of censorship. I guess they'd have a field day with this book.

And just what is this book?

Although Tiff will appear as a character here, this is not his biography. That important project is in hands far more capable than mine. Nor is this my autobiography. I will be using my life story sparingly, in much the same way my family once used a Christmas tree: as a framework upon which to hang favourite decorations. My decorations are anecdotes, stories with which I've peppered my conversations for decades. Stories of linguistic misunderstandings, those trammeled moments that can be highly comical, sometimes farcical and, occasionally, truly embarrassing — and of which I have been a collector, a perpetrator and, to be truthful, an addict.

As one of the more striking examples of the verbal traps that can catch anyone, I offer the following.

When Tiff and I moved to the countryside in Brock Township, we discovered that the local paper, *The Cannington Gleaner*, occasionally reported the news to appear more startling than it actually was. There had been a long wrangle between parents and the school board over sex education. The policy, when we first moved there, was that such training was the responsibility of the parents; teachers could not discuss such matters as part of the curriculum. Finally, though, things changed. Courses were set up, and, at last, the high school staff could talk about sex.

And how did the *Gleaner* announce this?

By an article headlined: "Cannington High School to Feature Oral Sex Education."

My goodness, we thought, how progressive. For perhaps a nanosecond. See what I mean?

My very first failure to communicate took place in the early 1930s, when I was still sleeping in a crib in the smallest room of my parents' cramped apartment. One dark night, I was suddenly awakened by the realization that I was not alone. There was only enough light for me to be aware of a long, cylindrical shape just beyond my blanket-covered feet. The shape was vaguely familiar — but not its behaviour.

I needed help.

I called out, as loudly as I could, the only word I could conjure to describe this invasion: "Sausage! Sausage!"

(Years later, I overheard my parents recounting this event to friends, telling them that their first reaction was "Oh, Lord. The little bugger's hungry again! What can we get him now?")

My father eventually appeared, and managed to remove the source of my panic. He then stayed with me, with gentle explanations, until I fell asleep again.

And so I learned an interesting new word: rat.

This signal event took place in the slums of Hamilton, Ontario, in the third year of the Great Depression. It was a time when jobs were hard to find and, for my father, impossible to keep. He was epileptic.

Now, this is not a rags-to-riches story — even though I had to learn, early, that a meal consisting of bread and gravy could be highly satisfying (especially if it included a special dessert treat: a sandwich filled with a mixture of brown sugar, butter and vanilla). No. I was blessed with more important riches: a loving family and, later, wonderful friends. Most of all, perhaps, there was language. A growing vocabulary, the wonder of shades of meaning, the fascination of how words had been derived. It was no accident that my eventual profession turned out to be writing, or that many hours of my adult life have been spent in teaching and editing.

Since my friends know me as a prairie type, they may be asking at this point, What was I doing in Hamilton, Ontario?

This is how it came about.

My mother had grown up in Regina, and had gone east as secretary to a Saskatchewan Member of Parliament. In Ottawa, she met a young man from Ontario's Bruce County and, after a time, they eloped to Chicago. Her parents were appalled to learn of this through a telegram sent by Mother's former boyfriend who, like her, was from Regina. They were even more upset when they were told of my father's illness.

We struggled along in Ontario for a few years, but ultimately had to throw ourselves on the mercy of my Regina grandparents. They had their own financial difficulties, but nothing as severe as what we were suffering. We moved to Regina when I was four — into a small bungalow rented by my grandfather, just across the back lane from his own large house.

In 1937, I entered kindergarten at nearby Davin Public School, named for Nicholas Flood Davin, the founder and editor of Regina's first newspaper, the *Leader Post*. (I remember bragging to my family that my class was the only one to have its own bathroom.) Then came 1939: memorable for the Royal

Visit of King George VI and his charming wife, the mother of our current Queen, and the outbreak of World War II. Memorable, too, for the break-up of the Whitehead family. My father retreated to Ontario and my mother and I moved in with her parents.

Nobody would tell me what epilepsy was. My mother tried to explain it away as "uncontrolled rage." My grandmother, a prominent Regina clubwoman, clung to the unfortunate notion that anything that afflicted the brain had to be seen as mental illness and, therefore, a regrettable scandal.

(Not surprisingly, she relished other peoples' scandals, particularly those published in *Hush* and *Flash*, which she smuggled into the house wrapped in the innocuous *Winnipeg Free Press*. I would sometimes take forbidden looks at them, and was puzzled over why so many people were being arrested for stealing sculptures. It was obvious what "statutory" meant, and the dictionary informed me that "rape" meant "to seize and carry off.")

My grandfather had nothing to say about my father's illness, even on those nights when he used to receive a frantic call from my mother and then, to the sound of banging pots and pans in the kitchen of our little house, bundle me up and carry me off to spend the rest of the night in the big house across the lane.

I didn't realize how much damage this secrecy inflicted until I was in my teens and took part in a high school visit to Calgary. At a dance that was meant to celebrate the completion of whatever it was that had brought us all together, one of the young male students from another school suddenly fell to the floor and went through all the violent horrors of the disease. The sights and sounds this involved were horrifying. The full impact of my father's suffering became vividly apparent — and just as bad was the feeling that I might inherit the same suffering.

Fortunately, that never happened, although everyone — including me — got a little edgy when, at the onset of puberty, I began to have fainting fits. Happily, they eventually stopped. The "silence policy" had also been maintained, years before, when my father moved back to Toronto. It was never explained — leaving me to conclude that he was simply seeking work in the east. I was never told of the divorce. I finally discovered its documents when my grandmother asked me to retrieve some papers from her carved oak desk. I resented being considered incapable of understanding the situation. Just as I resented the scene that played out as I moved each fall into the next level of public school. Every new teacher would have each of us stand up: "Give your name and tell us what your father does." All I could say about my father was "I don't know," which caused a lot of hurtful comments about how stupid I must be.

For the most part, though, I was incredibly fortunate when it came to my family. My mother somehow became more a big sister than a parent — more a friend. She was someone who bubbled with enthusiasm and energy. The only problem was that I didn't get to see a great deal of her. Once her marriage broke up — and World War II began — she got a job with the federal agency responsible for raising money through the sale of war savings stamps and bonds. Then, just as the war was ending, she became engaged to a Regina widower; they were married in 1946, when I was about to turn fifteen. From then on, I continued to live with my grandparents — except for the summer months, when they would spend much of their time at their summer cottage in the Qu'Appelle Valley, north of the city. In these times, I would move in temporarily with my mother and my stepfather, Stanley Thomson.

Whatever the benefits or drawbacks of either home, one thing was certain: I was extremely well fed. Both Mother and Nana were excellent cooks — as were most of the women of their generation. The fruit cellar in both houses always held abundant stores of homemade preserves and pickles. Every Christmas was awash with brandy-soaked fruit cakes, gift-boxes of delicious shortbread and assorted treats such as Chinese Chews (sweetmeats featuring dates and figs rolled in icing sugar) or chocolate-covered peanut butter balls. My grandmother's deep-dish apple pie had to be tasted to be believed.

Mind you, there was more than a touch of Anglo-Saxon snobbery in our cuisine. My grandmother refused to prepare my grandfather's favourite — corned beef and cabbage — because she thought it was deplorably "Irish." Mother was sickened by the very mention of Middle European flavours, such as that of Brussels sprouts. And yet they occasionally accepted — on my behalf — samples from our Serbian cleaning lady's kitchen, such as apple strudel and, believe it or not, cabbage rolls.

My high school days were a time when Canadian cuisine was changing drastically. For one thing, convenience foods began to appear (my lunches at home were awash with Kraft Dinners). And, before we knew it, old-fashioned recipes were being replaced by simpler dishes that took advantage of new groceries.

One of my mother's favourites was called simply "Crunch." It was made by covering the bottom of a buttered baking dish with the contents of a can of fruit pie filling. On top of this, cake mix would be sprinkled, enough for a one-layer cake. To this would be added two-thirds of a cup of sliced almonds and two-thirds of a cup of melted butter. Cooked at 350 degrees for forty-five minutes, this would produce something quite tasty — especially if served with an ice cream topping (but, alas, never with the wonder that once came from our old hand-cranked ice cream maker).

When I inherited my mother's personal, handwritten cookbook, I was delighted to find the dish outlined above — but less delighted to discover another way in which words can be deceptive: uncertain penmanship. One of our family favourites was a relish made with green and yellow beans in a savoury sauce. Unfortunately, in my mother's hand, an intended "ic" had taken on the appearance of a "u" — producing something I don't think I want to try: *Mustard Pukle.*

Tiff's mother had her own version of a "convenience dessert." The recipe began with the somewhat startling direction to "dissolve 24 marshmallows in a cup of boiling coffee." Then, when the mixture was cool, a cup of whipped cream would be stirred in, with the entire custard — in one bowl or in individual ramekins — topped by grated unsweetened chocolate. Again — surprisingly good.

Like everything else, though, the "convenience" notion grew to a deplorable degree. In today's supermarkets, have you ever tried to find a container of plain yoghurt? I creep along about fifty feet of shelves trying to find something without augmented flavour or added fruits. I am still appalled that walking from one end of a Stratford supermarket to the other means a journey of more than a city block!

One thing my mother did achieve for me was to see that I learned to type. When I was ten, she bought me an old used Underwood and a manual of typing exercises. I practised faithfully for months and became quite proficient. There was only one problem: I got bored with the whole thing before I had started to learn the upper row of keys — the numbers. To this day I am a skilled and rapid typist with no need to look at the keyboard, until I need one of the number keys. Then everything stops while I find the right one, hit it, and return to my rapid-fire typing style, until the next numeral.

Life with my grandparents also brought many adventures with words. They both wore dentures and were both hard of hearing. As a result, each suffered from slightly sloppy diction and frequent misinterpretations of what they heard. I would listen from my bed in a small upstairs den as they shouted back and forth from their respective bedrooms, which lay on either side of mine. One night, my grandfather called out to report on his latest appointment with the family doctor, who had apparently commented favourably on the excellent state of his patient's feet. My grandmother was appalled.

"Ridiculous!" she stormed. "Doesn't he know that they're false?" Instead of "feet" she had heard "teeth."

The exchange ultimately ended in a somewhat sulky silence, but morning brought reconciliation, especially when Grandad arrived with Nana's tea tray.

Such misunderstandings would delight me for the rest of my life, especially once I linked up with Tiff. In 1986, when he was president of English Canada's arm of International PEN — a writers' group similar to Amnesty International — he was a delegate to its annual international conference in Lugarno, Switzerland. And, as on all his travels, I went with him. The following year's event was to be held in Seoul, Korea, and so the head of the Korean delegation was invited to deliver the keynote address. His remarks would be based on the theme chosen for the event, which was — badly expressed in English — "Border Literature." This did not refer to writing achieved where England and Scotland meet, but was meant to be a plea that "writing should move freely across all political boundaries."

When he stood to speak, we were pleased that he was able to address us in English. Much of what we had witnessed up until then required simultaneous translation and, apparently, all the translators were rather proper English spinsters. Heated exchanges onstage were translated through our earpieces as mild statements such as: "I'm afraid I must express disagreement over what my honoured colleague from (wherever) is expressing." Well, by then, I knew enough French and German to be aware that what was actually being said was far stronger — and much more profane.

Tiff and I settled back and listened to the Korean's address. His English was good and his speech was just fine. Its problem was that there was so much that could be said on the subject at hand — only so much, and little more. Eventually, my mind wandered out of the conference hall to the shores of beautiful Lake Lugano, along the walkways that wound through flowering trees, blazing with gorgeous blues and magentas ... But, suddenly, my mind was yanked back into the auditorium. The speaker had grown loud and passionate — and his accent had become almost impenetrably strong.

This is what I heard: "Ladiesszz an' gentlemennn! Little Richard mus' not be confined! Little Richard mus' be freed!"

I turned helplessly to Tiff, signaling my confusion. Who the hell had Little Richard? And why?

Tiff leaned over and whispered, "Litter ... ratchur. Literature."

I started to giggle and only just managed to stifle my snorts and gasps. Otherwise, I'm afraid I would have disgraced Tiff, the Canadian delegation, and perhaps the whole nation of Canada.

NOW, BACK TO REGINA IN THE 1930s. My grandfather was a remarkable man. He was one of eight children in a family that had started out in Rawdon, Quebec, and slowly moved west. Most of his siblings ended up in Alberta, but Grandad stayed in Winnipeg and, at the age of twelve, started to work for his uncle, Jerry Robinson, who had a small department store there. That was where he learned about men's clothing, starting with a laborious count of the number of stitches per inch in the various fabrics used in that trade. He had been good at arithmetic in school and picked up enough about business and accounting at his uncle's place to be able, eventually, to open his own store in the new settlement of Regina — less than twenty years after the town's founding in 1882. That was when the Canadian Pacific Railway reached a former native settlement known as Pile-o'-Bones, named for the piles of bison bones left over from the inhabitants' hunting.

He was both a quiet and caring grandfather. He would take me to the movies every Wednesday afternoon, the day on which all Regina businesses closed at noon. He would regularly take me to the public library, so I could select my next Edgar Rice Burroughs while he sought out his Zane Greys. He would also let me count the coins in his ancient cash register at the end of the day, when he was making up his daily accounting. In later years I found one just like it in an antique store and bought it. My original plan was to convert it to a repository for flatware and keep it in the dining room, but it's still in my bedroom, holding spare keys and other small essentials.

My grandfather apparently met my grandmother when she was still a girl. She grew up near Winnipeg. They encountered each other on the wide prairie, each of them on horseback, simply riding on the open plains.

By the time I knew her, the Victorian lass had passed through years as an Edwardian belle to become a prominent Regina clubwoman — slightly eccentric and, to be honest, more than slightly snobbish. She somehow managed to link my grandfather's Robinson family to an ancestor named Lord Rokeby Robinson, and soon used his family crest and Latin motto on her personal stationery: *Non nobis solum sed toti mundo nati*, which I would try to translate as "Creation is not only for us, but for the whole world."

Words to live by.

Nana, as I knew her, was the first woman in Saskatchewan to achieve a driving license. She was a tireless volunteer with the Children's Aid Society, having weathered encounters with knife-wielding drunks and wild-eyed prostitutes. Like my mother, she was more of a friend to me than a relative and, in many ways, the closest friend I had. Many evenings, we would lie across her bed in the dark, enjoying our shudders as we listened to such delightful radio horrors as "Inner Sanctum" or "The Shadow" — me in my flannel bathrobe and Nana in her black satin lounging pyjamas, embroidered with huge gold-threaded dragons.

Many of my friends today find it difficult to believe just how innocent we all were in the days of my youth in Saskatchewan — an innocence prolonged, in part, by the generation gap between me and my grandparents.

Humour, in our house, had not the slightest whisper of sex. Much of it was based on simple wordplay. I recall with great fondness the naïvety of the jokes I revelled in during those days. Many were nothing more than fragments of dialogue:

DINER: Waiter! What's that fly doing in my soup?
WAITER: (Leaning over to look, then straightening up) Ah ... the backstroke, I believe, sir.

The restaurant was a favourite milieu for humour:

WAITER: And how did you find your steak, sir?
DINER: Oh, easily enough. I simply moved my mashed potatoes ... and there it was!

We all howled at that one — especially my classmate, Dick Irvin, who would one day be one of Canada's leading hockey broadcasters.

Then, there were other snatches of dialogue:

HE: Do you hear that? What's making that noise outside?
SHE: (listening) Herd of cows ...
HE: What do you mean! Of course I've heard of cows!
SHE: No, no. A cow herd!
HE: Well, I don't care. I haven't said anything a cow shouldn't hear ...

And in act two of this fragment of theatre of the absurd:

HE: Hey! I like your shoes. What're they made of?

SHE: Hide.

HE: Hide? Hide! Why should I hide?

SHE: No — no. *Hide*! A cow's *outside*!

HE: So what? I'm not afraid of any old cow!

In fact, in my family, the one potentially forbidden subject about which jokes could be made was urination.

My grandfather was a Director of the annual Regina Exhibition. Every year, on the midway, there was a machine visitors could use to fashion a gag "identification badge" — a small flat metal circle that would be embossed with a name. Uncle Leyton would use it each year to make something that, under certain circumstances, could be given to the driver of a car by one of his passengers. The ring would bear this important message: PEE TICKET; STOP AT NEXT BUSH.

Mind you, on those great flat open plains around Regina, bushes could be few and far between.

It was also my uncle who told me my first joke. He started in on an elaborate story about a fabulous bedroom with a bed that had something wonderful above it. He pretended to have forgotten the name of that something. I, eager to show off my growing vocabulary, walked right into his trap by proudly offering "canopy." His reply: "No, that was under the bed!"

It took a moment. And then I got it. Can-o'-pee.

One of the most daring of such plays on words could be found in the public toilets. On the prairies they were sometimes labelled POINTERS and SETTERS.

I suspect that this one limit on expression in my youth may explain why so many of my anecdotes have to do with urine. My first adult encounter with the comic possibilities of that subject comes from the University of Saskatchewan, where I ultimately took two degrees in Biology, with a special interest in entomology, the study of insects.

Senior courses involved insect dissection — a delicate process that soon presented a problem. I began to develop a luxuriant growth of warts around my cuticles, which severely hampered delicate procedures.

I went to the campus doctor to see what could be done about this. As it happened, the university had just set up its first radioactive facility, which was centred on a cobalt bomb. It was being used to treat all kinds of conditions; it was decided that it should be tried out on my warts. Thus, gingerly, I stuck the tips of my fingers into its radioactive field and hoped for the best. It did, indeed, have a marked effect on the warts. They turned dark and grew even bigger.

The next assault on my warts was with the help of a drug called something like bismuth subsalicylate — a heavy white liquid that required a very large syringe for injection. I embarked upon this second set of treatments, and soon learned from a friend in the pharmacy department that it had once been used in the treatment of syphilis. An amusing fact I mentioned in passing to one of my fellow biology students, Evelyn Ching.

Now, since the campus doctor's offices were in the medical building, I used to get my injections during the only class I took there, which was a weekly biochemistry lab. We had reached that point in the course in which we were to do a series of analyses of our own urine. Evelyn was my lab partner in that class and — with the exception of us and one fellow biologist named Al Ewen (but known to all as Jughead, because of his huge ears) — the class was made up entirely of pharmacy students — all of them, apparently, deeply religious, to judge from their attitude towards those of us from the questionable realm of biology.

Evelyn herself came from a similar background, having taught at an Anglican school for girls. For one of our urine labs, she was forced to do what everyone did who was unable to provide enough material for individual analysis: she had to take a beaker, go to a washroom and wait for someone who might oblige. The first person she encountered was one of her former students. She interrupted the student's delighted greeting with a stern: "Never mind — just go in there and fill this up for me!"

That week, there we were: thirty people in one room, each boiling a little metal pot of urine until it crystallized and could be analyzed. The atmosphere in the room was, to say the least, heady. Hot, malodorous and steamy.

When the nurse came to the doorway to wave me out for my injection appointment down the hall, I failed to notice her. Someone, however, did.

Jughead.

"Hey, Whitehead!" he yelled out. "Your syphilis shots are ready!"

All the proper pharmacists peered through the yellow haze at me.

I knew it must have been Evelyn who ratted on me, so I swung around to yell at her: "This is your fault!"

Whereupon the pharmacists, misinterpreting, switched their disapproving gaze to Evelyn. She, in all innocence, wheeled to point at Jughead. "Well, he started it!'"

I escaped into the hall, rushed to the clinic, dropped my trousers and was duly injected. For the rest of the semester, biochem lab — for the three of us — was a chilly event.

The injections didn't work, either. It wasn't until I had left both science and Saskatchewan that the warts immediately disappeared — for good.

A few years after my "syphilis caper," I received my MA in Biology and took a break from my studies to work at the University Hospital in Saskatoon. Occasionally, I would serve as a human control in some experiment being run by a colleague there. When a comparison was needed of the metabolic rates of humans and rats, I and a lab rat — for some reason named Elvis — would simultaneously swallow a small, chocolate-coated pill of blue dye; and, later, the precise time the dye first appeared in our urine would be noted.

Something happened, however, that proved distracting. Two years earlier, I had applied for a job with the British Colonial Service — to study the tsetse fly (the carrier of sleeping sickness) in the Gold Coast (now Ghana). Suddenly, there was a call from the Service asking me to have a medical examination that very day. I hurried down to the same office in which I used to get my "syphilis shots."

The thought of Africa was so exciting that I forgot all about the blue pill. I rushed over, was poked and prodded and bled — and then given the usual beaker and the usual request: that I retire behind the modesty curtain in the corner and deliver up a urine sample. Not even then did I remember the experiment Elvis and I were involved in. Not, at least, until I filled the beaker with a brilliant turquoise fluid.

I emerged to deliver my sample to the young lab assistant who was waiting to analyze it. I think she was quite new to the job because, before I could explain about Elvis, she grabbed the beaker and ran into the next room screaming: "Muriel! Muriel! What the hell do I do with this? It's *blue!*"

In the long run, the Colonial Service resumed its slow and ultra careful pace — so much so that by the time they wrote to offer me a job, I no longer had either the wish or the need for it.

Then, years later, when I was working in Toronto as a freelance writer of documentaries for CBC Radio and Television, I developed kidney stones, an ailment with sudden and extremely painful attacks.

At that time, I was a regular guest on a radio show hosted by Helen Hutchinson. One day at the microphone, I was hit by utter agony. Fortunately, Helen was talking at that moment, and managed to keep going as I slid from my chair to the floor. With great aplomb, she suggested we have another piece of recorded music, and signalled frantically to the operator in the glass booth. Fortunately, the music lasted long enough for me to get most of the pain under control and we got through the rest of my segment.

Later attacks lasted longer. By then, Tiff and I were living on an old farm northeast of Toronto. When the worst attack of all hit, my doctor insisted that I be booked into a hospital in the nearby town of Lindsay.

It was the middle of winter. The ambulance that took me to Lindsay was barely able to make the trip; in fact, it would be a week before the next vehicle was able to get out of our neighbourhood.

Settled in my ward, I gratefully received an injection of morphine. A brisk older lady arrived with papers for me to sign. What papers? Well, the authorization for my surgery. What surgery? The papers would explain all.

I read that I was about to undergo "cystoscopy and basket removal." Basket removal! Now, I had by then encountered many actors from Britain. (One of my Canadian actor friends had once exclaimed: "Oh, to be in England, now that England's here!") And so I knew that in Britain, a man's "basket" was his genital bulge.

I begged her to tell me what "basket removal" entailed, but all she could say was that I'd have to ask my doctor. When could I do that? She didn't know; he was trapped somewhere else by the blizzard.

Eventually, I had the surgery, having learned that the ominous expression referred to a little device attached to the fibre optics thing that would be inserted into the urinary system through the penis — and the "basket" could be opened and closed to trap whatever stone or stones might be sighted.

Surgery was done. No stone was discovered. I was sent home, wiser and sadder.

What I ultimately discovered, of course, is that words can become even more dangerous when different languages are involved. For example, there's an encounter I had with a urologist in France, where Tiff and I had established a small writing retreat on the outskirts of a Provençal village called Cotignac. Shortly after we bought the place in 1995, it was discovered that I had cancer. Fortunately, it was not too threatening: a malignant polyp on the inner wall of the bladder. Upon our return to Canada, it was easily removed and all would be well — as long as I underwent an annual examination that involved inserting an optical instrument into the bladder, retracing the path taken by the surgical devices through my penis.

Back in France, I found a urologist whose clinic was about

forty-five minutes away from Cotignac, and made an appointment. Having suffered kidney stones as well as bladder cancer, I was quite accustomed to the ways of urologists. Usually, at the beginning of the appointment I would be handed some kind of small receptacle, in the hopes that I would use it to provide a urine sample. After my forty-five minute drive, I was somewhat overprepared to do so. To my consternation, *Monsieur le Docteur* did not require a sample. In spite of my protests — and with the help of two strapping Provençal nurses — I was divested of my lower clothing and plopped into the stirrups. The stirrups! I protested: "*Monsieur — je dois uriner!*" To no avail. "*Desolé, monsieur, je me depeche!*" ("I am behind schedule.")

Now, you have to know that in Canada a local anesthetic is administered in such circumstances — by simply dripping the appropriate liquid onto the target area. Not so, I discovered, in France. The doctor picked up one of the largest hypodermic syringes I had ever seen and calmly filled it. The look on my face betrayed by feelings. And so, although he didn't speak English, he trotted out a reassuring little phrase he had apparently learned for the comfort of his Anglophone patients:

"Ah, monsieur — just a little prick!"

And he stabbed me with the thing.

My revenge was immediate. I was laughing so hard I couldn't explain why — and, with that, I peed wildly all over the place.

Now, back — at last — to growing up in Saskatchewan.

There was some confusion over the exact ages of my grandparents. The village church in Grandad's Quebec birthplace had burned down, destroying all the parish records. He knew that he had been in Winnipeg during the Riel Rebellion and, a year or two later, had started work in his uncle's store at the age of twelve. Working backwards, we assigned him a birth date of 1874. With my grandmother, the confusion was a matter of vanity. Her birth had been noted in the family bible, but at some point, the date had been scratched out and written over, presumably by her. The new date was 1881, and she was not at all pleased when I noted that she must then be just a year older than Regina.

My grandparents survived the infamous Regina Cyclone of 1912 without injury. Grandad's brand new Reo car did not fare so well. As one of the few motorized vehicles in the city at the time, it was pressed into service as an ambulance, which did unspeakable damage to its upholstery.

At that time, my grandparents were living in a huge house with a barn in the backyard, where my mother kept her girl-hood pony. I used to pass the place every day on my way to high school; it was situated on a street that afforded a lovely view of the new Legislature, across what would become Wascana Park.

Once, as Tiff and I were leafing through one of his family's photo albums, we came across a shot of the Saskatchewan Legislative Building. He said it had been taken by his grand-parents when his grandfather, Thomas Findley, then president of Massey-Harris, had been on one of his tours through the prairie provinces. I was flabbergasted. I could tell from the angle and distance involved that the Findleys could well have been standing in front of my grandparents' house! I couldn't help but imagine my grandmother, inside, pulling aside a curtain and musing, "Who are those people?"

Today I have younger friends who seem to think that for someone such as me — having grown up with all the privations of the Depression and wartime rationing — youth was a sad time. This wasn't so. Not at all. It was wonderful. Saskatchewan has been referred to as "Next Year Country" — a place of optimism, with the common belief that whatever the economy or the weather might inflict on us, next year it might be better. Lives built on hope can be wondrous.

I often think of a four-line verse that I have always assumed was written by Ogden Nash. No. The author, I discover, was someone with an incredible name: McLandburgh Wilson.

> Twixt the optimist and pessimist
> The difference is droll:
> The optimist sees the doughnut
> But the pessimist sees the hole.

For someone with a growing interest in insects, life on the prairies in the Dirty Thirties had fascinating features. Ordinarily, cricket and grasshopper populations are kept manageable by the prairies' spring rains. Every year, enough insect eggs in the soil would be drowned, thus preventing population explosion. But the drought of the thirties allowed several years of spiralling survival rates. Ghastly for the farmers, but exciting for me. We would drive out of town to experience firsthand the solid mass of insects streaming across the highway — which would soon become almost impassable as the slippery corpses piled up. And then there were the caragana beetles — little black insects that fed exclusively on the caragana hedges decorating almost every Regina garden. I remember being told that hordes of the beetles were approaching from the north; two days later, there was not a single caragana leaf left in the entire city.

My insect fixation took many forms. One of my grandfather's sisters-in-law, Jean, used to make frequent trips from Alberta to Regina to visit. I called her my "flying aunt." (Aunt Jean's daughter, Merle, was once elected Queen of the Calgary Stampede. The press took only slight notice until, shortly before the annual event began, Merle Robinson got married — to a man named Stier.)

There are certain cautions any insect-lover has to learn through painful experience. Lesson One for me was delivered when, as a toddler, I tried to pick up a wasp I had discovered as it ran across the lawn in the backyard. I was soon howling in agony. My grandmother quickly consulted the family doctor book, the source of hundreds of home remedies and — after a quick visit to the stem garden at the back of the yard, where we grew asparagus and rhubarb — she applied the proposed treatment for an insect sting: rhubarb juice. It worked; it was such an interesting remedy that it managed to distract me until the pain of the sting subsided.

(One of the most intriguing remedies in the doctor book was the treatment recommended for frostbite: "Take the skin of a freshly killed rabbit and apply it, fat side down, to the afflicted area." Where on earth, I wondered, did one find a freshly killed rabbit?)

Lesson Two happened when my family and I made one of our annual early summer visits to the Qu'Appelle Valley to pick Saskatoon berries. Dried, they were a major component of native pemmican — and, baked into a pie, they offered a delicious combination of the flavours of cherries and blueberries.

On one such foray, when I was about twelve, I found a particularly abundant supply of the berries on one huge bush. I was able to fill two of the honey pails I was carrying, especially when a low mound beside the bush offered me a way of reaching higher than usual.

I soon discovered, however, that the low mound was an ant hill: the home of huge and aggressive red ants. Before I knew it, they had swarmed up my legs and into my underwear.

My resultant screams brought my family running. The pain was so terrific and so shocking that I can't remember exactly what was done. Yet I recovered and, yes, remained fascinated by such creatures, even though I was appalled that all these "social insects" could exhibit such agonizing "anti-social" behaviour.

I swore never to get too close again to anything small that might sting or bite.

A highlight of my youthful interest in wildlife was when I became caregiver to a family of baby robins. A pair of the birds had nested in a fir tree in the backyard. I used to watch the parents pulling up earthworms from the lawn and then feeding them to the loudly hungry chicks. Unfortunately, though, a pair of English sparrows built a nest just under the robins' home and dismantled it in their search for building materials. When I found the robin chicks on the lawn below, I provided them with a new home in the form of a small square peach box filled with shreds of excelsior. This I set out in a quiet corner of the garden, and was delighted to see that the cries of the baby birds soon attracted the attention of the parents, who resumed the feeding of their young — but with one exception. The runt of the brood was tossed out of the nest. I tried putting it back, but to no avail. I set up another peach box nest in the garage, and took on the task of feeding the orphan myself with occasional help from my mother. I wouldn't advise it. It was an endless task. Fortunately, the beginning of summer had released me from school, so I was put on worm-digging duty, while my mother supplemented the live diet with bits of bread soaked in milk. I don't know why Mother thought this appropriate for a wild bird, but the bread — offered, as were the squirming worms, with the help of tweezers — was eagerly accepted. Mother, like me, became very fond of the little orphan.

The young robin survived and grew. The only problem was that its ordeal seemed to have affected its voice. All that came out was a high, hoarse "peep-peep." Not surprisingly, we named the little creature Peep-Peep.

This had consequences. That was the summer during which the vacant lot next door was taken over by new neighbours. Their house was completed by the time our pet robin was flying and they moved their belongings in through their backyard from the back lane. Meanwhile, we were still offering food to our robin. With me off at school, it was my mother — then working only half days — who did most of the feeding. She would go to our back screen door with a saucer of moistened bread and start calling.

Imagine our new neighbours, whom we had barely met, carrying a heavy box through their backyard. Suddenly, the screen door of the neighbouring house bangs open and a diminutive figure bursts out — Mother was not much more than five feet tall — bobs up and down, and in a high, piping voice like some bizarre version of a cuckoo clock starts crying: "Peep-Peep! Peep-Peep!"

I hope there was nothing breakable or valuable in the box in our new neighbours' hands, because down it went, while father and son watched in amazement as a full-grown robin flew up and landed on Mother's head.

At the age of twelve, thanks in part to my interest in nature's wonders, I became the youngest member of the Saskatchewan Natural History Society. The next-youngest member was sixty-eight.

The Saskatchewan Natural History Society was essentially a group of elderly birdwatchers who got together twice a year. The first gathering was on December 25, when we would all trudge through the snow of Wascana Park, trying to spot any feathered friend foolish enough to brave a Saskatchewan winter. It was called "The Christmas Bird Count."

The count was seldom high.

The other event was held in the spring — the Annual Banquet. The meal, catered by the local ladies of the Canadian Legion, was always good. Too good, in fact. Most of my aging fellow birdwatchers would eat too much, too quickly. Digestive upsets were frequent and occasionally dire. One of the Legion ladies developed a helpful tradition of leading us all in postprandial exercises. These were brief, vigorous and accompanied by a recitation we were required to learn by heart. I remember one of them, during which we would slap various parts of our bodies with names similar to words in the script:

I (EYE) say! (MOUTH) Have you heard (EAR) about Harry (HAIR)?

Well, Harry (HAIR) just (CHEST) got back (BACK) from the Front (STOMACH) where he was needed (KNEES) at the foot (FOOT) of the Army (ARMS). Hip! Hip (HIPS)! Hurray (ARMS IN THE AIR)! For Harry (HAIR).

At this point, most of us would sink gratefully — if not too gracefully — into our chairs.

This little performance haunted me for the rest of my life. When Tiff was writing his first play, which was set in an asylum for the insane, he started looking for some exercise the inmates would be asked to do, during which they would all get it wrong — leading to utter chaos. I was foolish enough to mention my memories of "Harry." Tiff and his director at Ottawa's National Arts Centre, Marigold Charlesworth, both thought it offered great possibilities. And so I was recruited to teach the cast its simple routine. By the time Marigold and Tiff got through choreographing the mayhem, it proved so popular that, during the performances, they often had to do an encore.

Fast forward to the early eighties. I was asked by the CBC to rescue a television project that had been abandoned by its producer. It involved editing a lot of musical footage, shooting new footage, and giving it all a political flavour that would please both the star and his audience. Since I had never before been involved in television musicals, I have no idea why I was chosen to do the job — but it was just bizarre enough to be an alluring challenge. Added to which was the identity of the star, an artist whose work I loved: Harry Belafonte.

I met Harry in Toronto, during his tour of Canada. He proved to be as charming a colleague as anyone might expect. During the process, we became good friends. I eventually took a technical crew down to the Caribbean island of St. Martin, where Harry had a house. He had been told that if he appeared in the country of his boyhood — Jamaica, where shooting was originally planned — a recent change in political leadership would threaten a lot of violence, with possible danger to him and us. This provided some difficulty for me — a documentary writer — because shooting on St. Martin meant that we had to pretend it was Jamaica. We found a small house that would serve Harry, on camera, as "the house I was born in," and a small school that he said was "the school I attended."

It was all more like a holiday than work, yet we got all the shooting done and it looked good. And I stayed with the Belafontes in their huge beachfront house.

One evening, with the help of a few large and powerful Belafonte pina coladas, I recounted my childhood adventures with the birdwatchers, and found myself standing before Belafonte, his family and his friends performing "Harry."

That was a mistake. Not that they didn't like it. They loved it. And that was the problem. During my week's stay, I had to repeat the damned thing every night, for every new set of visitors. By the time it was over, I never wanted to "hear about Harry" again.

Most of my brushes with greatness, however, were second-hand. During my childhood, such encounters usually involved my grandparents. It was my grandmother who got to meet Queen Marie of Romania. And now, one of my most cherished possessions is a large brass samovar inscribed with the Romanian royal crests. When I show it to visitors, I usually quote the famous Dorothy Parker piece:

> Oh, life is a glorious cycle of song,
> A medley of extemporanea;
> And love is a thing that can never go wrong;
> And I am Marie of Romania.

Queen Marie of Romania became a popular figure in western Canada during the twenties and thirties. She had a Canadian

lover who had become rich in the Klondike Gold Rush — Joe
Boyle — and used to make "royal progresses" across the country.
On one of her visits to Regina, my grandmother, as head of the
local chapter of the I.O.D.E. (the Imperial Order of Daughters
of the Empire) was in charge of the afternoon tea arranged
in Marie's honour. A few weeks later, the Queen's thank you
arrived in the mail: the samovar.

Another indirect connection came through George Robinson,
my grandfather's brother. He ended up in Calgary, where, in his
early days, he shared law offices with a young man who was
destined to become Canada's prime minister: R.B. Bennett.

When World War I broke out, young George Robinson
enlisted and was eventually invalided out of the army. He had
been emasculated by shrapnel. With what I like to think of as
"prairie practicality," he came home and married a lesbian. Thus,
I came to know Great Uncle George, with his booming sense of
humour and bristling military moustache; Great Aunt Eleanor,
with her mannishly short silver hair and pin-striped suits worn
with a shirt and tie; and her live-in companion, Great Aunt Ted,
a very quiet woman whose name was actually Edwina.

When R.B. died, he left a little money to his old law buddy,
George; George was next to go, and included Bennett's bequest
in what he left his wife, Eleanor; when Eleanor died, her only
heir was her companion, Ted — who, with no family of her
own, decided to divide the money among Eleanor's nieces, one
of whom was my mother. By this time, Tiff and I had just bought
a run-down fifty-acre farm about an hour and a half northeast
of Toronto. It would ultimately become a gorgeous country
estate known as Stone Orchard, but at that time it needed a lot
of help and a few essentials.

A letter arrived from Regina. It contained a cheque for two thousand dollars and an explanation from my mother.

"… and so, since I don't really need it, and you probably do, here it is, with love. Who knows, you might have some urgent need …"

Indeed we did have more than one urgent need. Our ultimate decision, however, was to use the money to build a swimming pool in the backyard. Before moving to the country, we had occupied a house in Richmond Hill, north of Toronto, owned but not yet occupied by Tiff's parents. We really missed the pool situated in its garden.

When the Stone Orchard pool was completed, we began telling friends it was The R. B. Bennett Memorial Pool. In consequence, the pool had two notable visitors.

One involved a young historian who visited the place and, noting the new solar heat system that had been installed, observed: "That's a bit bizarre, isn't it?" What did he mean? "Well," he said, "don't you know that R.B. died when he was unable to get out of an overheated bath?"

The next visitor was one of my colleagues at *The Nature of Things*, the well-known environmentalist John Livingston. He seemed vastly amused, which would prove to be a bit dangerous. Not long after his visit, we drove to a neighbouring community to pick up an old friend for a weekend at our farm. While we were gone, John Livingston paid a secret visit to Stone Orchard, and in the flower bed that bordered the pool, he planted a small professionally fashioned sign identifying the swimming place as a Bennett memorial.

When we arrived back with our visiting friend, the first thing she saw when entering the yard was the sign.

"Take me home," she said. And meant it. To her — another Westerner — R.B. Bennett had been guilty of creating the Depression that almost brought down the country.

It took half an hour of argument and a couple of strong drinks — plus a temporary removal of the sign — before the guest was persuaded to stay. Her name was Margaret Laurence, cherished as both writer and friend.

I did actually get to meet a future Prime Minister of Canada, briefly, when I was still a child. Before my grandparents bought a lakeside property north of Regina, on the shores of Last Mountain Lake in the Qu'Appelle Valley, we used to rent a nearby cottage at Saskatchewan Beach. It was right on the water, with terraced gardens cascading down the valley side behind it. It was my job to keep them watered, with hose pressure arranged by having a big tank up at the top of the hill and a heavy motorized pump down at the shore. Once the water was pumped up to the tank, gravity would drive it down through the hose or into the plumbing in the house.

One day as I was watering, I became dimly aware that something was going on at the cottage next door. A lot of cars were arriving, and people were pouring down the path that lay just the other side of a wire fence, separating it from our place.

My total attention was soon grabbed by the sight of something I had never seen before: a huge butterfly bobbing through the air. It was my first sighting of a Monarch. I turned, fascinated, to watch its progress up the hill, not realizing that my move redirected the water from my hose. Suddenly, there was a roar of protest. I swung back, facing the fence, to see a tall, furious figure with beady eyes and tight, wavy hair. I stammered some kind of apology, which resulted only in the figure stomping away.

I learned later that the local Conservatives were having some kind of meeting at the cottage next door. The man's name was John George Diefenbaker.

Those summers at Saskatchewan Beach were enchanting, except for a period I would love to forget: when I became a wanton and cold-blooded killer. After my grandparents had bought their own cottage property, my grandfather bought me a BB gun. The minute I held it, I wanted nothing more than to kill something.

I went down along the shore, where a "Dirty Thirties" labour project had constructed stone riprap to support a series of terraces that gradually climbed the valley side. All day, mice threaded their way over the stones, and frequently following them would come a small weasel. Here, I knew, I would find something to kill. In less than an hour, I had slaughtered four mice and the weasel.

I next turned my attention to the big, open sliding doors of the boathouse. I knew that bats spent their daylight hours up in the hollow of the doors' track. All I had to do was stick the muzzle of the gun into the crack and pull the trigger. Soon, the bats were silent. I had a pile of small corpses at my feet.

What else could I kill?

I changed into my bathing suit, retrieved a pitchfork from the garden shed and waded out into the shallows of the lake. Given the high clay content of the soil, the lake bottom was a deep, silky mud, rich in iron and sulphur. Your feet sank several inches into it and came out both smelly and stained black and yellow.

It was among the reeds that swayed above the shallows that certain large fish would forage for food. They were large and dark. Some people called them suckers; others, carp. For whatever reason, in my family they were known as buffalo fish.

I stood stock-still in the shallows and waited for the sight of dark dorsal fins and tails, swirling the surface of the murky water. Yes. Close. Closer … Strike!

With some effort I lifted the heavy, writhing body to the shore, where I used a heavy stone to finish it off.

I knew enough to remove the fish's scales, head and tail. I then carried it into the kitchen, where my grandmother looked deeply doubtful but agreed to cut it up and try cooking it.

It was ghastly — redolent of the chemical content of the mud. Even the cat refused to eat it.

(We learned later, during the War, that a small commercial fishery started up just down the shore from us — concentrating completely on buffalo fish. The fish were netted, slaughtered, canned, and cooked. During that period of meat shortages, it was sold as "White Salmon — Guaranteed not to turn pink in the can.")

Some of the buffalo fish scales had stuck to my skin, and my grandmother saw just how they could be used.

Most of the ladies of her generation were deeply involved in various crafts — china painting, rugs hooked out of dyed raw wool. (I helped with the carding, and once pulled a pot of dye off the stove, severely scalding one arm in my attempt to see what was cooking.) Then there was stamen jewellery — brooch and ring forms, plastered with a special kind of putty into which coloured stamens made of plastic could be arranged to form patterns. My mother's specialty was wood carving and embellishing picture frames with heavy pewter or copper foil, then beating graceful floral patterns into them. And there were shell pictures: floral prints onto which small sea shells and fish scales — bleached, dried and tinted with watercolours — were affixed to give the prints a three-dimensional look.

My blood lust was harnessed to benefit my grandmother's crafty friends. I speared and scaled all summer, washing and bleaching the scales and drying them on the sun-drenched dock. Buffalo fish scales, it turned out, made perfect rose petals.

My hunger to kill? It suffered a setback the morning I caught my first-ever sight of a garter snake, slowly wriggling across the lawn. I ran in, grabbed by BB gun and began to shoot. The snake was too quick for me — so I ran up to it and began to beat it to death with the stock of the gun. The snake finally died, but not before the wood of the stock was irreparably cracked.

I tried to be philosophical. After all, I'd had a good go at it. And so, sadly, I gave up on the gun.

A few weeks later, a strange thing happened. I was exploring the valley slopes above our cottage when I heard a weird, rhythmic sound: a repeated, gurgling croak. I crept to the source of the noise and discovered a crow, injured in some way I never discovered. It had a broken wing and a cut on its neck. With every croak, the bird twisted its neck and blood came out.

I stared in horror. I knew I had to put the poor thing out of its misery, but I no longer had a gun.

Finally, I did what I had seen my grandfather do when, out hunting prairie chicken, he discovered a wounded bird. I grabbed the crow around its neck and whirled it around my head until the croaking stopped.

Its neck was broken and my hands were covered in blood.

I ran home, crying, and hid in the boathouse for what seemed hours. I vowed never to kill another animal.

(Talk about naïve. As you will learn, during my university years, I killed thousands. Literally, thousands.)

In a sense, though, my boyhood encompassed the days when killing was almost universal: World War II.

The war, to someone living in the middle of the continent, seemed very remote. I was not acquainted with a single person in uniform. All the war meant to me was a series of auxiliary activities. I was among the thousands of kids hauling our little wagons around our neighbourhoods, collecting anything that might support The War Effort. Metal coat hangers; silver foil from packaging, every piece separated and then rolled up into a big ball; honey pails, usually filled with leftover cooking fat; newspapers; and, at Halloween — given the shortage of sugar and the resulting lack of candy — we all collected coins to add to the Milk For Britain fund. At school, boys and girls alike knitted coloured squares of wool that would be sewn together by the girls to form afghans to be sent overseas. My knitting partner was a war guest — one of the children evacuated from Great Britain and sent to the dominions and colonies for safety's sake. I look back with amusement that the very first British person I met — my knitting partner — was named Pamela Bland.

Through those war years, Regina families were supposed to make a show of their patriotism. I was charged with picking baskets of flowerheads in the backyard, and using them to form a huge sign on the front lawn — a large "V for Victory," with the Morse code for "V" placed below it: dot-dot-dot-dash. My grandfather put together a huge "V" of lightbulbs mounted on wood to hang above the front door. My grandmother was quite upset when that sign was joined by another, smaller one beside the door. Thanks to me, it read: "German Measles."

There was one wartime project in Regina that was to have a profound effect on me. My grandmother was on a committee converting an old apartment building into a home for war guests. They were especially proud of its library — a huge collection of children's literature, much of it British, including several years of *Boy's Own Annual* and *Chums*. The trouble was that by the time the place was finally ready, the war had ended.

It ultimately became a home for the blind; as for all those books, the committee simply divvied them up and took them home for their own youngsters. And so, suddenly, I was inundated with kiddy-lit, none of which I had ever read before. I became fascinated by Dr. Doolittle and his ability to talk to animals, and with Tom Swift and his wonderful inventions.

There was something beautifully ironic in my first encounter with children's literature coinciding with the onset of puberty.

Let's face it. In so many ways, I was anything but sophisticated. These were simpler times, but certainly my experience of them was simpler than most. Being brought up by Victorian grandparents and a working mother — while at the same time having few close friendships at school (I was a "brain") — meant that I was incredibly naïve. I actually finished public school without discovering the important anatomical difference between the sexes. I gained only some hazy idea that reproduction entailed the passage of some vital material from one sex to the other through the conduction of their "sex organs." I was puzzled about how this was actually achieved. Did the boy and the girl each hold their penises together, using the foreskin to form a channel for the delivery of whatever it was?

Honestly, it was that bad.

I was hopeless when it came to knowing the meaning of dirty words. I overheard two of my seventh-grade classmates talking about one of the female teachers "waddling down the hall with her ass wiggling." I had somehow gained the impression that almost any dirty word had something to do with the penis, so I was puzzled. How could they tell her penis was wiggling, given that she was encased in a corset and a dress?

I suspect it was the family doctor book that finally corrected my immature ideas. In addition to home remedies, it contained anatomical drawings. Although they were skilfully drawn and beautifully coloured, they managed to look more like engineering plans than body parts. I may well have sought out what lay below the waist in both sexes — and thus, perhaps I finally became aware of that organ with a name so startlingly similar to that of my home town, Regina.

I simply didn't have the vocabulary shared among my contemporaries. I had no idea what girls were talking about when they coyly used code words whose initials spelled out an apparently forbidden word: "Father. Uncle. Cousin. King."

I was not only ignorant of the words; I was also ignorant of some of the activities to which they referred. At public school, there were two extremely close friends — a grade or two ahead of me — who had reputations of being exceptional scholars, as well as being a bit odd. I remember the day — during recess — when they threw me to the ground and pinned me there while they asked me their question of the day. I was asked to define a certain word. I had never heard the word before, but it sounded a bit like philatelist, which I did know. I meekly asked: "a stamp collector?" For some reason, they found this very funny. And I guess I would have, too, if I had then ever heard of fellatio.

(I remember in later years, when one of the fellows won some impressive scholarship, the lady who introduced him tried to give a sense of his erudite childhood by maintaining that when he played with his toy train, instead of "choo-choo" he would chant "masticate-masticate!")

It wasn't that my family didn't try to face up to its educational responsibilities. I remember, at fourteen, coming home at noon to have lunch and change my books, and discovering on my way up to the attic, which had become my newly acquired teenage digs, the same family doctor book, lying open on the stairs. Its revealed pages displayed two photographic portraits: one of a handsome and sprightly young fellow, another of a dissipated, drawn, pimpled and warted individual. Looking more closely, I discovered that these were "before" and "after" portraits of the same person. Gosh! I started to read, but failed completely to discover what had caused this ghastly transformation. The piece seemed to be about something called "self-abuse," but at no time was there any hint as to what that might be.

I took the book downstairs to where my grandfather was just finishing his lunch and asked him what the heck this was all about. That was when I received the only sex education of which my family was capable. My grandfather grabbed me by the wrist and said, "Bill, you must ... you must never ... Ohhhh ... You must always ..." at which point he burst into tears and ran from the room.

Now, you have to appreciate just how bizarre my fourteenth year was. There I was, in my first year of high school — only a few months after having discovered that girls didn't have penises — and revelling in my first contact with stories meant for much younger children. And it was at that very moment that I launched into my first highly charged sexual affair.

I had fallen in love with a classmate. A male classmate. There is neither need nor willingness to go into any detail. Suffice it to say that he initiated the relationship and that it was entirely satisfactory to both of us. It proved no deterrent to his having girlfriends and, ultimately, a happy marriage — and, for whatever reason, it went happily on for over five years, right into university days. It was a lot more educational than any Victorian article on self-abuse!

I came to suspect that a lot of experimenting went on between male adolescents. It was easy and it was safe — no pregnancies; it fostered a sense of confidence and comfort about the sex act; and it didn't have to imply perversion or any kind of permanent practice. Best of all, it could come to an end whenever either chose such a thing — with (you should pardon the pun) no hard feelings.

That, I believe, describes the motives and part of the behaviour of my own private friend. Why did it go on for so long? I have no idea. We started out as friends and we parted as friends. What else matters?

Wiser friends, in later years, had plenty of suggestions to make about my own attitudes to and practices of sex. Starting at the age of eight, they noted, I lacked the male role model usually provided by a father figure. I spent more time with female relatives. And (something I find more amusing than important) when I was nine, I briefly had to wear female attire.

I caught chicken pox. Given the timing of its onset, the burning question for me was: would I be allowed to go downstairs on Christmas morning to open my presents? The family doctor was consulted. His suggestion: yes, I could go downstairs, but only if I protected the lesions by wearing a pair of my mother's silk stockings. (It was my first time, but not my last. I've always been said to have shockingly attractive gams.)

It's true: I neither had, nor sought, much male companionship. My best friend was a girl I met in kindergarten, Jean Howard. Her father was one of my English teachers, and her mother taught me to weave when the newly elected Canadian Commonwealth Federation government reintroduced crafts to the curriculum.

(Whatever opinions are held about Saskatchewan's socialist party — or about its offspring, the NDP — I am deeply grateful to have grown up in the province that enriched its school curricula and that introduced socialized medicine to Canada. Mind you, I am quite aware of contrary judgments. Even in my time, members of other parties were dismissive of our provincial government. This was a time in which there was a rash of jokes featuring Little Alice, who was always ready with a wry, amused comment on current life. For example: Little Alice was taking a cross-Canada flight when the pilot's voice came over the intercom: "We are now flying over the virgin prairies of Saskatchewan." Little Alice just laughed. She knew what the CCF had done to Saskatchewan!)

Yes, simpler times — especially for me and my friend, Jean.

When we were just old enough to have learned to print, we used to play Post Office. Now, unknown to us, most of our classmates who played it collected kisses as postage. Not us. We would close the door leading from her parents' dining room into the bedroom hall, and equip ourselves with blank envelopes and pencils. Then, with each of us on opposite sides of the closed door, we would take turns slipping an addressed envelope under the door, waiting for another to be slipped back.

Amazingly, we could spend many happy hours playing our ultra-simplified version of the game.

Jean ultimately married one of her law professors, Charles Cole. They had two sons. I used to babysit the elder, Frank, shortly after his birth. I was then working on my MA and would take my microscope and specimen slides to the Coles' apartment. Never once was my work interrupted by any sound from the baby. In later years, Frank became a well-known cinematographer who, tragically, was murdered by brigands while he was filming his solo crossing of the Sahara Desert on a series of camels. Although we are still friends, I no longer see Jean. Age and memory loss have robbed her of any knowledge of who I am. I miss her terribly.

Most of the kids on my street were girls. The only other boy shared my name. He was a few years younger and at first he referred to me as "Other Billy." The rest of us, older, used to form scratch softball teams and play in the vacant lot behind one of the houses across from mine. The family — the only Catholics I knew — was named Street, and their red-headed daughters were always on my team. I smile, now, at the memory of how much and how often we all talked, in perfect innocence, about the "Street girls."

The simple truth, of course, is that as long as I can remember I've been attracted to males — however much social pressures caused me to simulate relationships with females. To me, this is simply who I am. To any outraged heterosexual who condemns me for having chosen an unacceptable lifestyle, I would simply ask, "And at what point did you choose your lifestyle — and on what basis?"

If you want facts and figures, here goes. In my lifetime, I've tried four times to establish a lasting relationship with some- one of my own sexuality. Two of these were utter failures and short-lived. One involved sex for only a short time during its beginnings. It, however, was extraordinarily successful, lasting forty unbelievably rewarding years and ending only with death. Does that tell you something about Tiff and me? Our sexual personae were simply too different. It wasn't a matter of who did what to whom, it was in our whole attitude towards the sex act and, for instance, in how many hours might be needed to prepare for it.

As for fully sexual friendships with heterosexuals, there were six. One — already noted — starting in high school and proceeding into university days; one following soon after, and lasting throughout much of university. Four developed while Tiff and I were living at Stone Orchard, completely, I hope you understand, with Tiff's knowledge, while he pursued his own brand of things — which seemed to be a preference for strangers. None of my affairs lasted less than two years. One went on for eight. How can that be? I have no idea. The others always had girlfriends. There was even a wife or two. In at least one case, the wife knew and didn't seem to mind.

Given that Tiff and I seem to have been viewed by some as poster boys for gay marriage, I suppose I am obliged to say something more about the real nature of our relationship.

We loved each other, and fashioned lives together that were both magical and productive. What were we to do about our sexual incompatibility? We were both practical and intrinsically honest. Deception was out of the question. And so we found that each of us could follow his heart, which meant diverging sexual lives, and we could still remain a happy and functional couple.

It wasn't as difficult as it might at first seem.

For one thing, work occasionally took one of us away. In the mid-seventies, for example, Tiff lived in Ottawa for six months as playwright-in-residence at the National Arts Centre. And, when he returned to our rural home, I left for Ottawa to spend over two years as Assistant to the Director of Theatre at the NAC.

With frequent visits back and forth, the arrangement worked out well, giving us each the freedom to do what we needed to do. And then there was almost a year during which we added a major, two-storey wing to our house. For that time, Tiff moved across the road to the second farm we had bought in order to escape the loud distractions of construction. The increasingly sprawling nature of our home base made sexual independence all that much easier to maintain.

To be honest, there were some touchy moments. No marriage is without them. In the long run, however — and for the most part — we made it work, thanks to bonds of love and collaboration on shared goals.

But, that's enough of that. Let's talk about something else.

I've told a fair amount about my grandparents, but not so much about my mother and father. In some ways, the most significant thing about Mother was that, just after World War II ended, she remarried. Stan Thomson, fifteen years her senior and a man who had already been widowed twice, with children from each marriage.

Unknown to me, shortly before the marriage was announced, my family got together and decided that I would need some special distraction in order to cope with this new development. (As I later discovered for myself, the marriage was not viewed with favour by my grandmother. She was old-fashioned enough to find three wives, whatever their fate, to have been two too many. She never accepted my mother's new life and never welcomed my stepfather into her home. Sad, but that's the way it was.) The distraction decided upon was something I had longed for, begged for, but never received: a puppy. My earliest memories of my grandmother included a series of cherished Fox Terriers, each of them, as I recall, named Paddy; but, for some reason, there were now no dogs in my grandparents' house. That was about to change. It was decided that the best dog for me and the household would be small: a toy Boston Bull Terrier, to be exact.

He was incredibly small and irresistible. With a complete lack of imagination, I decided to call him Tiny.

As a pet and a companion, he was marvellous. I dashed home from school every day to be with him. Weekends were heaven. I was not without friends, but now I had a friend who was totally available.

Over the next few months, Tiny grew out of his puppyhood and, before long, he was larger than any toy breed. Soon, he was larger than a regular Boston Bull. I didn't care. I adored him.

And then, one day when I returned from school, I couldn't find him. Nobody was at home. Tiny wasn't in the garage, where he usually spent time if the house was empty. When my grandparents returned from wherever they had been, I tearfully told them about my missing friend.

They already knew. To my horror, my grandmother explained: "He wasn't what he was supposed to be, so we had him put down. Your mother agrees. It's the right thing to have done."

Put down?

Killed. Because Tiny wasn't as tiny as he should have been.

I eventually recovered and made a stab at forgiveness, but that's only part one of this story.

Part two didn't happen for about forty years. By then, I was living on our farm in Cannington. Tiff and I had two dogs — lovely, big Malamutes — and what seemed like acres of cats.

One day, my parents arrived as they usually did, unannounced, all the way from Regina by car. Unannounced, but not unaccompanied; my mother was carrying a full-grown but incredibly small Chihuahua.

Fortunately, I had not had to go to Toronto that day, but was working at home, finalizing a script. Tiff was at his desk, starting his next novel. We both stopped work and got my parents and their new pet settled in the guest room. Since we had not planned on company for supper, we decided to take everybody out to a favourite restaurant in Beaverton, about ten miles to the north.

The five of us — Tiff, me, my parents and the little dog — entered the dining room, to be met by the owner. I made the necessary introductions, and the owner made a necessary suggestion.

"Mrs. Thomson, unfortunately, by law, I cannot have a pet in the dining room. But I want you to know that I will be happy to look after her in my office. I have a doggie bed there, and a food dish and a water bowl. I'm sure she'll be quite comfortable."

My mother became glacial. "Where I go," she said, "the dog goes."

I tried every argument I could think of to persuade my mother to see reason, but to no success. Eventually we had to drive back to the farm, where we dined on scrambled eggs and toast. The meal was eaten mostly in silence. Finally, I felt I had to say something.

"Mom, that was ghastly. There was nothing he could do. It's the law. I'm sorry, but I think you behaved very badly."

Her reply was something I will never forget and something that changed our relationship for the rest of her life.

"Bill, with me, the dog comes first. Before everyone."

After a silent evening and a silent next morning, my parents and their little dog got into their car and left.

"With me, the dog comes first."

Well, there's just one more thing you should know about that incident: the dog's name.

It was Tiny.

Perhaps it's safer to take the story back to Regina, to high school days.

First, there was the fire. I was playing tennis at the school courts in the late afternoon, when my mother drove up and urged me to go home: to my grandparents' home, because it was early fall and they were back from the cottage.

She explained that the house had almost burned down.

When I got there, I discovered it was only my own area — the attic — that had suffered fire damage, although water from the fire department's hoses had done a lot of damage to the rest of the house.

What on earth had happened? My grandmother had asked

me just that morning if her seamstress could use my oak library table as a surface to iron the slipcovers she was making for the living-room furniture. Apparently, the poor seamstress had gone to lunch, leaving her iron plugged in and on while it sat on the table. The iron burned through the wood, fell against the room's fibreboard wall and set aflame the wood shavings that insulated the attic.

In response to this news, I opted for discretion. I had a hazy memory of rushing up to my room after my lunch in order to pick up that afternoon's textbooks — only to discover that the seamstress had unplugged my radio/gramophone in order to plug in her iron. In a hurry to get back to school, I plugged my music source back in and left. Could it be that I had started the fire accidentally by plugging in her iron? Yes, I suppose it could.

And that provides a glorious irony. (No pun intended.)

According to my grandparents' wedding anniversary celebrations, they were married on New Year's Day, 1897. I was often made to wonder just what preceded that original event, since — all through my growing up — New Year's Eve was the one time my grandfather would get helplessly drunk and would have to go to bed. My job was to sit up with him all night, making sure that whenever he sat up to have a cigarette he didn't burn the house down.

See what I mean?

My grandparents moved into the Hotel Saskatchewan, where they would stay until all the repairs were done — which included not only rebuilding the attic, but also replacing the plaster and hardwood flooring on the lower levels, through which the fire-dousing waters had flowed. It was nearly Christmas before the house was ready for reoccupation. Then, sadly, the night before the planned return, a plumber's assistant forgot to turn something off and the bottom two floors were flooded all over again, delaying everything until spring.

If I was indeed responsible for starting the fire, it took only a week or two before happenstance provided a punishment.

By then I had moved to the south side of Wascana Creek, to spend the rest of the summer living with my mother and stepfather while my grandparents summered at the family cottage in the Qu'Appelle valley, moving back into their restored Regina house by the time autumn arrived.

At that time, it was a teenage fad in Regina to fashion your own personal cannon out of inch-and-a-half iron pipe by stopping up one end and drilling a hole into the side. You then mixed charcoal, sulphur and potassium nitrate to form a kind of gunpowder and poured your powder into the open end of the pipe, having already inserted a wick into the hole in the side. Then, using an iron rod and some cotton waste, you forced some tamping down onto the powder. You then set the loaded cannon on the ground, lit the fuse and ran.

The best site for an ear-shattering explosion was just a block from my grandparents' home and only a few blocks from my mother's. Here there was a tunnel that ran under the north end of Albert Street Bridge. It was to the tunnel I went with two of my friends who came to collect me, saying they had built a new monster cannon out of two-inch pipe and wanted to try it out. Off we went. Fuse in, powder in, cotton waste tamped down with the iron rod, fuse lit. Suddenly the universe exploded. The noise was shattering. We ran. We ran as fast and as far as we could.

I realized later that one of my friends had had a very narrow escape. The tamping rod in his hand was shot out of the pipe with great force, just barely missing his head. As for me — well, after about a block, I became aware that running was not easy. I then discovered a hole in my left shoe. Not in the sole — but in the upper, and blood was pouring out. The explosion had sent the two-inch pipe down, through my foot, until it hit the concrete floor of the tunnel and bounced out again.

When my friends caught up with me, we decided they would help me home, where I would go upstairs, clean up in the bathroom, get rid of the tell-tale shoe and all would be well.

All was not well. My parents were entertaining that evening. I was discovered, crawling on hands and knees across the hall floor, leaving a glistening red trail behind me. With true Regina courtesy, my parents introduced me to their guests ("How do you do? How do you do ..." from the floor) and called an ambulance.

I was in the hospital for three months. Gangrene set in. Doctors and nurses came every morning with a little pot of acid to burn away the foot flesh that had died overnight.

Apart from the hellish medical matters, it was a heavenly sojourn. School friends came and brought thoughtful (or misguided) gifts. One guy brought me two pin-up calendars from the recently ended war — one by Petty and one by Varga. They proved very useful. I copied the lush young bathing beauties onto sketching paper, using coloured pencils and pastels, but put the nurses' faces on each one. They became collector's items throughout the hospital. Once I got onto crutches, I prepared lunches for the night staff. And with a walking cast, I was given a brief instruction (with an orange as the target for my syringe) which allowed me to take over the penicillin rounds on my ward. (In the post-War days, hospitals were run much more casually than today!)

I loved it. I kept up with my homework, and in the long run — unhampered by teachers of various qualities — I ended up with an eleventh grade average of 98.6 per cent. On the downside, I had to give up my brief career as an amateur figure skater. My left foot was no longer strong enough to carry me across the ice.

THE FINAL IMPORTANT EVENT IN MY high school days came when I was finally able to reconnect with my father — by which I mean I at last had a chance to reintroduce myself to him.

I was a member of a high school organization started by the YMCA — a Hi-Y Club — and was sent as a delegate to the group's national conference in Toronto. My father had unusual Christian names — Berkeley Kyle — and so was easy to find in the Toronto directory. I knew contacting him meant going against my Regina family's wishes, but I wanted to see him again.

I took the Queen streetcar all the way out to his Queen Street East address, where I nervously knocked on the door. After a few moments, it was opened by a dark-haired woman whose body was terribly twisted — a hunched back and short, tormented legs. She said: "Yes?"

For a moment, I was speechless; then I managed: "Uh … is … is Mr. Whitehead in?"

She turned and yelled: "Berk!"

As she moved away, she passed a total stranger walking towards me. My memories of my father centred on a tall, slim man with Black Irish colouring: jet black hair and bright blue eyes. Approaching me was a short, stout man with white hair, wearing grey trousers and a white undershirt.

"Yes?" he said, as he reached me.

I was speechless. "Uh ... I'm ... Bill ..."

"Bill who?" he demanded.

"Oh ... your ... son?"

We had a glorious reunion: lunch, reminiscences and, later, a visit with one of his sisters, Norma, whom I remembered well. (His other sister had married a former leader of a political party in Ontario — Walter Thompson. I remembered visiting their farm near Pickering, Ontario, now part of that town, and riding their massive Newfoundland dog.)

My father's second wife's name was Hilda. She had been badly injured in an automobile accident. They had met in an orthopedic ward, after he had taken a seizure on the lakeshore and slid, feet first, down a concrete embankment and broken both his heels. Towards the end of his life, I was happy to learn, his epilepsy was finally brought under control.

I would get to see my father once more, when I travelled to Toronto for yet another national conference two years later. Then, just as I was finishing my Master's thesis, I would receive a letter from Hilda, telling me that he had died.

Exits and Entrances

*I*t was a foregone conclusion that I would go on to university after completing high school, but nobody was sure — least of all, me — just where that would lead. Through much of my childhood I had dreamed of becoming a deep-sea marine biologist, thanks in large part to *National Geographic*'s thrilling reports of the work of Dr. William Beebe in his bathysphere. But it dawned on me that becoming a marine biologist would mean spending a lot of time in water — very deep water. Something not found in Saskatchewan, and something the very thought of which terrified me. I wasn't much of a swimmer, and couldn't execute much of a dive. I was never comfortable being out of my depth. So goodbye to marine biology.

I still vaguely believed that I might become somebody who could be paid to learn about animals, particularly how they behaved and why — especially insects, in spite of the pain they had inflicted on me. And so it was entomology that was in my mind when I enrolled in the University of Saskatchewan.

The main campus of U of S was in Saskatoon, several hours to the north, but in those days students from the southern regions of the province could achieve their first-year studies in Regina. This was made possible by the local affiliate of the U of S, Regina College, which was located right across the street from my former high school. The college served students not only from Regina, but from other southern Saskatchewan communities.

This was to be the site of one of my early adventures with organized religion.

A few weeks into our studies, the dean of the college called a few of us Reginans into his office. It seemed there was a problem concerning one of the student bodies, the Student Christian Movement. That year, SCM membership was made up entirely of out-of-town students. The dean did not want them to feel that the locals were ostracizing them and suggested that he would greatly appreciate it if some of us would show up for at least a couple of their meetings.

By this time, I had abandoned any relationship with any religion. I had done this partly because all beliefs, however beneficial they might be to human society, seemed in my estimation to have been completely fabricated. I had finally been excused from attending my grandparents' church, an Anglican pro-cathedral — which meant that it was High Anglican, with services that borrowed much from the Catholic Church, including candles on the altar, genuflection and a lot of kneeling.

It was the kneeling, plus whatever was going on in my body during adolescence, that did me in. During Lent, the Litany was seven pages long: seven pages of continuous kneeling. For three years in a row, at the same point in the service, I fainted. I can still hear that moment in the service. The minister would say: "The Lord be with us." The congregation would respond: "God be with us." And then we would all intone: "Christ be with us."

Blackout.

Each year, for three years, I came back to consciousness with four strong men trying to retrieve me from my fallen position — firmly wedged between pew and kneeler. (It was not an easy task; I was a chubby child.) My next awareness was of the ceiling of the church, swaying, as those four strong men carried me up the aisle and out into the fresh air.

It was hardly surprising that the minister and his assistant (named to my delight Reverend Cole and Reverend Wood) suggested to my family that perhaps services were not appropriate at that stage in my life.

In spite of all this, my conscience persuaded me and two of my friends to attend one of the SCM meetings. We were warmly received by our fellow students from neighbouring communities.

Too warmly. They elected me president. Oh, Lord ...

On one of my grandmother's principles ("In for a penny, in for a pound"), I accepted the post and braced myself for future meetings in which I would probably feel like a hypocrite.

Then, I made a startling discovery. I had not known that Regina College had originally been a Methodist institution and that some Methodist procedures were still active there — such as the ten-minute chapel service, held twice a week. And I certainly didn't know that one of these weekly services was to be led by the President of the Student Christian Movement.

After consideration and trepidation, I concluded that I could do it — as long as I approached the whole thing as theatre. I would perform the role of a Christian, a Christian leading a Christian service. There were actually a few moments of the performances that I began to enjoy, and so, it seemed, did some of my friends who came to watch. Then, one day, I got carried away. I worked myself up into a climactic moment in which I triumphantly assured my audience that if they did "this," "that" and "the other thing" — "It will fill your soul with hope!"

Unfortunately, what came out was: "It will fill your hole with soap!"

Pandemonium. My friends burst out laughing. One of them, doubled over with mirth, ran from the room.

I concluded the service as best I could and resigned from my SCM presidency, with apologies.

But my resignation did not come into effect until I fulfilled one other duty of the president, which was to act as one of Saskatchewan's delegates to the annual international Congress of the SCM, which was to be held in Toronto. (This gave me my second and last opportunity to see my father.) There, I had two further examples of the treachery of words.

The first came when I took a break from the meetings to visit the men's room. I think it was the only time in my life during which I stood at a urinal, giggling helplessly. From within one of the closed stalls there came a quivering, somewhat absent-minded rendition of "Nearer My God to Thee."

The second event occurred during one of the meetings. At all of them there were official delegates taking an active part, along with a few observers from other countries, all of whom had been warned that they were not allowed to enter into any of the discussions. This rule was, if you'll pardon the pun, religiously observed — until, during one particularly contentious exchange of opinions, a female observer from Britain could not contain herself. She rose to counter loudly whatever had just been said. A fellow observer — he was from China — immediately leapt to his feet to protest that she was out of order.

"Mary ... Mary ... you are ... you are ... Illegitimate!"

ON ONE OF TIFF'S BOOK TOURS, we were housed on the McMaster Campus in Hamilton, in the president's residence. Since the current president's family was too large for the place, he was living in rented quarters off campus, while the residence was used as a guest house for visiting dignitaries.

One of our fellow guests was an Anglican cleric from Britain. I believe his name was Dr. Robinson, who was famous for having written serious books on the subject of Christian belief, with titles that hinted at more profane utterances. The first one was called *For Christ's Sake* and I think there was another, *In God's Name*. According to the housekeeper, who served us an early breakfast, he had even more interesting aspects to his life.

"Oh, he's a very nice man. Very nice. But you should see what he keeps in his closet! Frocks! Gorgeous, they are — all lovely brocades and velvets. Oh, my. There are a couple I wouldn't mind having myself! But, for goodness sake, don't tell Dr. Robinson!"

We didn't have the heart to explain ecclesiastical vestments to her.

It was reminiscent of something I once saw on a cinema marquee — apparently advertising a cross-dresser's double bill:

"Jeff Chandler in *The Tattered Dress* and Bob Hope in *The Iron Petticoat*."

(Speaking of street signs: how about these two I once spotted — actually on separate establishments but, as seen from up the street, appearing to be linked: "JESUS SAVES" — and, just below — "WHY DON'T *YOU* SAVE — SHOP HERE!")

In the fall of 1950, having completed my first year studies, I moved up to Saskatoon. I enrolled in the College of Arts because the courses it offered covered two disciplines, the arts and the sciences. It would allow me to follow my main interests, which were in biology — animal behaviour, especially the behaviour of insects and other invertebrates. By then, however, I was also interested in another aspect of animal behaviour — human behaviour — and this took the form of theatre. Thus, while my first degree would show a major in biology, it would also show a minor in theatre.

My undergraduate days were heaven, particularly my courses in entomology under a remarkable teacher, Jacob Rempel; he fostered and developed my curiosity about bugs. But my undergraduate years also taught me a lot about people.

My Regina days were spent mostly with WASPs, white Anglo-Saxon Protestants. The student body in Saskatoon, though, was about one-third of Ukrainian descent — the result of an early twentieth century immigration policy that peopled much of our prairies with arrivals from those parts of Europe where dry land farming was practised. There were few representatives, however, of other races. (In my day, Regina had no blacks, few Chinese people and only one Japanese family.) One year, in Saskatoon, when I went to the campus accommodation office seeking somewhere to room, I was asked if I would find it acceptable to share a place with a black student. The question amazed me. Of course I would. (Apparently there had been quite a few who wouldn't.)

My roommate for a year was Kwame Buahen from the Gold Coast (now Ghana). He was tiny, very dark, congenial and, according to his first name, born on a Saturday. We got along very well, sharing a two-burner hot plate and a bed, but Kwame was having a tough time with the rigours of the prairie winter and — as a vegetarian — with the usual winter shortages of fresh fruit and vegetables. I would watch in fascination as he prepared the same meal, every evening, all year, without exception. He boiled rice and made a sauce of fried onions and canned tomatoes, to which he would add an egg.

It was wonderful, years later, to encounter him again — a doctor, practising in Thunder Bay, where Tiff and I had gone on a promotional book tour.

I taught for a bit in Saskatoon — not in the classroom, but in student laboratories. There was one biology course that all non-science students were obliged to take, and I was put in charge of its laboratory periods. With so many students to be accommodated, there had to be several of these labs each week; I had to hire assistant instructors.

I was given a tiny office in the biology building, into which, one day, two female students came. One was tiny, pallid and, as I would soon learn, hardly ever spoke. The other was tall, wearing a crocheted top, down the front of which a bit of egg yolk had dribbled.

She did speak.

"*Agathavan vierson tripund avriliasmuk.*"

I blinked and finally said, "I'm sorry. I speak only English."

The tall student looked impatiently at me. "I am Agatha Van Vierson Tripp, from the Netherlands, and this is Avrilia Smuk. She is Ukrainian. Who are you?"

"Bill Whitehead," I answered with a nervous smile that soon faded because Miss Van Vierson Tripp burst out laughing.

Seeing the look on my face, she explained: "In my language, your name means zee vurst part of zuh behind!"

We finally got it all sorted out. They were applying for jobs as my assistants and, I must admit, they worked out very well. We even became friends.

I soon discovered, however, other language pitfalls — in English. Some of the labs did not require active teaching behaviour. They would be set up as demonstrations: a whole series of microscopes, each with some kind of biological material mounted on a glass slide, each accompanied by a typed card that gave the identity and significance of the material. One such lab was titled Vectors of Human Disease. All the slides held specimens of small creatures whose lives involved the transmission of many of our diseases.

It was into one of these labs that a particular student came, who caused me a certain degree of embarrassment.

Her name was Sister Monica. She arrived, enveloped in a massive habit. She was the first nun I had ever met. Every time I addressed her as "Sister," I sounded — to myself — just like a Chicago gangster. I tended to avoid her. This time, however, I couldn't. She reached one of the microscope stations and read its explanatory card. Up went her hand.

"Oh," I thought. "Wouldn't you know it?"

She was at the station that featured the pubic louse. Crabs.

Nonetheless, I went over to her and asked: "Can I help you, Sister?"

She was very sweet. "Mr. Whitehead, I think there's a typographical error here." (I was not pleased. I had done the typing.) "Oh, well, could you show me?" She smiled and pointed to the name by which the creature is more properly known. "Should this not read 'the public louse'?"

There was no way out of it. I had to explain — to a nun — about the pubic area of our bodies, how the louse is adapted for clinging to those coarse hairs and how lice are usually transferred from human to human.

Sister Monica handled the situation much better than I did. She remained smiling and interested; the moment passed.

Shortly, there would be further adventures. I was quite enjoying the fact that, for the first time in my life, I was being addressed courteously as "Mr. Whitehead." One day, however, as a new batch of students arrived, I heard the sudden exclamation "Billy! Is it really you?"

It was my sixth-grade teacher, Miss Sullivan, and she was accompanied, believe it or not, by my seventh-grade teacher, Mr. Chisholm. They had both taken a year off to begin work on another degree. We had a cordial reunion, and I always looked forward to their friendly presences in my labs.

I was, however, having other problems. Few students showed much ability to cope with the spelling of scientific terms. I became so frustrated with this that I set up an unusual test — one that might drive home to the students just how unobservant they could be. In preparation for one of the labs that would include my former teachers, I went to the blackboard and wrote out a list of ten questions. Beside the questions, I wrote out their ten one-word answers, correctly spelled and in the right order. When the lab began, I told the students of the test, and assured them, truthfully, that all the answers were correct.

"I will now give you just sixty seconds to complete this test."

They all looked quite confused.

"Seriously. Just write down the answers. Starting now."

When the class was done, I announced that they would receive their marks the following week, and that the right answer, misspelled, would be considered wrong. Then I gathered up their papers.

I don't remember the exact failure rate, but I do remember that neither Miss Sullivan nor Mr. Chisholm passed the test. It was embarrassing for everyone.

Some of my university adventures were amusing; others, I must admit, were shameful. For example, there was the undergraduate summer when the Biology Department arranged to have me work on a provincial fisheries project in the Qu'Appelle Valley.

I was part of a three-man crew housed in the attic of a fish hatchery. The job of the other two was to set out gill nets late every afternoon, harvest the catch and collect scale samples (to show age) and stomach contents (to show diet and state of health) on a predetermined number of each species caught.

That operation was not without its problems, one of which I shared in: a fish hatchery, with so many water and air pumps running twenty-four hours a day, seven days a week, was an extremely noisy situation in which to try to sleep. It took weeks to get used to the constant uproar.

Then there was the size and range of the catch. Local fish

populations were booming. More species than expected — and some huge fish to dissect — meant a messy, bloody job. On top of all this, the catch — dissected or not — required disposal. The nature and amount of the garbage was daunting, especially given our failure to convince the locals to take advantage of the food possibilities of the undissected leftovers in the catch. Everyone was convinced that "those scientists" had done something unsavoury to the fish they offered.

What was I doing while all this was going on?

Oh, Lord.

I was put on something called "creel census." I was given a twenty-foot freighter canoe, equipped with a thirty-horsepower outboard engine, and told to patrol a chain of three small lakes in order to determine the size and nature of the catch achieved by local anglers.

Given the fact that I had never even been in such a large and powerful craft, let alone tried to navigate such a beast, this is what would happen: I would spot some fisherman out in his boat, roar up in my huge contraption and as often as not ram right into him. I was not yet good at judging when to reduce my speed. After profuse apologies, I would try to extract detailed information from him. How long had he been out today? What bait or lures was he using? How many fish had he caught? Which species?

It's hard enough to pry information from an angler under the best of circumstances. It's extremely hard when everyone I approached thought I was a game warden, eager to prosecute for lack of a license, illegal methods or too large a catch. My dismal boating skills made the whole process almost totally unproductive.

In the long run, I simply gave up. I explained to the head of the crew what my problems were and spent the rest of the day in the hatchery attic.

To make matters worse, I carried another burden of undone labour, left over from the previous weeks in Saskatoon. I was co-editor of the yearbook, and although the text was ready for the printers, page after page of student photographic portraits were not. The photographers had been late in delivering the hundreds of prints, and so I had brought them with me to Qu'Appelle, along with all the tools I needed to mount them on large sheets of cardboard.

I became so depressed over the horrors of creel census that I couldn't bring myself to complete the portrait layouts.

Eventually, I packed everything up and returned to Saskatoon, where I faced the fury of the head of Biology — and that of the president of the student council, once he discovered that the yearbook would not be available until months after the next term began. It was the worst summer of my life.

I am always happy to remember an earlier one that was much better.

After my year at Regina College, I was hired by Saskatche-wan's Department of Education as a clerk, assisting teachers in overseeing the departmental examinations — summer tests for students whose yearly average marks had fallen below a certain level. It meant a lot of work before the tests were writ-ten: bundling up the exam papers and sending them out to centres all over the province. Once the tests had been graded by a special committee of teachers, the resulting grades were recorded and a few "bonus marks" were doled out that might make the difference between passing and failure. During the actual writing of the exams, though, we had absolutely nothing to do.

Our supervisor, a large girl who looked remarkably like a blond Marlon Brando in drag, had a lovely sense of humour and a generous nature. Instead of wasting her time and ours on make-work projects, she led us up into the great dome that tops Saskatchewan's Legislature, where we all perched on the steps of the spiralling metal staircase while she read aloud to us.

The complete *Sarah Binks*, that lovely send-up of literary biography, written by a Winnipeg biochemist, Paul Hiebert. To this day, it is one of the most treasured volumes on my shelves, the story of a simple Saskatchewan farm girl who wrote atrocious epic poetry ("Up from the Magma and Back") and translated European classic poetry according to whichever foreign language textbook salesman had seduced her that summer. From the German, she translated Heine's lovely little gem, "*Du bist wie eine Blume*" — usually given as "As a flower, thou art," but in Sarah's hands: "You are like one flower." And using German word order for the opening of the second stanza: "*Mir ist, als ob ich die Hände Auf Haupt dir legen sollt*" she offered "Me is as if the hands I on head yours put them should."

Unkind friends still tease me about Regina being known, in the book, as "the Athens of Saskatchewan."

Our free time gave me an opportunity to take a look at ancient records, in which I discovered that although my uncle Leyton had been an excellent student, my mother just managed to pass from grade to grade.

Was it shameful to snoop? Probably, but little harm was done.

Throughout this period, nobody in my family viewed either my present activities or my possible future with much approval. My grandfather had hoped that I might take over his men's clothing business. My grandmother urged me to study law and achieve her own unachieved ambition — to become a judge. My mother hoped I might become a doctor. They all showed a degree of uncertainty about the possibility of my becoming a husband and a father.

They were not alone in this.

In spite of ample evidence to dissuade them, I still had friends who insisted on trying to link me up with a girlfriend.

One such attempt took place in the university cafeteria, which was situated in the basement of the women's residence of the Arts Faculty. I always found the place to be quietly amusing. One of my courses was a survey of American literature, including Hawthorne's novel about an adulteress, *The Scarlet Letter*. This is why I grinned at the fact that every female Arts student had a white sweater emblazoned across the breast with a scarlet "A."

Frankly, the cafeteria was just a basement: concrete floor and walls, heating and plumbing ducts and a series of wooden picnic tables that were used by bridge players outside of meal times. Each pair played either side of the centre of each bench, leaving room for a kibitzer at either corner.

One day as I was playing, a friend — who turned out to be one of my most fervent matchmakers — brought along his latest offering and installed her in the kibitzer's position beside me. I nodded cordially and continued to play. Now, I'm not a good bridge player, just as I'm no chess player at all. I could never see the sense of expending so much mental energy on a pastime. But that day, I bid and actually made a grand slam — for the first and only time in my life. Beaming at my partner, I reached to my left to shake my new acquaintance's arm, exclaiming: "Well, what do you think of that?"

She seemed at a loss for words.

I had reached just a bit too far and was vigorously shaking her right breast. I couldn't think what to say or do. All that came to mind was: "Would you like to go the Arts Ball next week?"

And so we started dating. I liked her. She was good company. We went to a fancy dress ball, dressed as two anatomically correct octopuses. (I had a removable tentacle. In nature, it would have been the male's sex organ, to be given to the female for her to use whenever her eggs were ready for fertilization.) Unfortunately, on the way to the dance floor, my sex organ was stolen by a mischievous waitress. Nevertheless, we won prizes for our costumes; each of us received a small travelling alarm clock.

The whole situation eventually got out of hand. One night, out in her car, I ran out of conversation. Taking her head in my hands (secretly hoping, I guess, she would not hear me) I proposed to her. She heard me. She breathed: "Oh ... yes!"

We spoke to her parents. We began looking at rings. It was ridiculous. I was deeply into a hot relationship with a young man in another faculty.

Finally, as tough as it was, I came clean. I told her what was what. She was wonderful. Sympathetic, understanding and, I was sorry to discover, heartbroken.

I swore never to dissemble like that again. And I never did.

THE FIRST HOSPITALIZATION SINCE MY CHILDHOOD tonsillectomy was in order to have my appendix removed — by a surgeon who afterwards complained rather petulantly that, in spite of the pain I had been experiencing, the organ appeared to be perfectly healthy. (I later suspected that the pain had been caused by kidney stones, from which I was ultimately told I was suffering.)

Two other events occurred during that hospitalization. I was bored, as surgery was delayed until I recovered from a severe cold, and so I decided to try an experiment. I had been told that as an infant I was allergic to bananas. Was I still? There was only one way to find out. I ate a banana.

I think I gave new meaning to "projectile vomiting." After my bedding and hospital gown had been changed at least three times — and the floor around my bed cleaned up — I confessed to what I had done. I thought the nurses were going to kill me.

But what the nurses failed to do, the surgery almost did. The procedure of giving me a spinal anaesthetic went awry. For some weeks after I left the hospital, I couldn't remain upright for more than half an hour without a severe headache developing, one that responded only to about an hour spent lying flat on my back. And that was about to be quite a problem.

By then I had attained a BA, and was about to start working on my Master's degree. My subject: the musculature of a species of spider. This topic was suggested partly because it would complement the research my supervisor, Dr. Rempel, had done on that species' embryology — and partly because I wanted to overcome my unwavering fear of spiders.

My subject was the most poisonous species known to science: the deadly black widow.

At first, I tried collecting specimens in the wild — black widows are fairly common in the extreme southwest corner of

Saskatchewan, in the Cypress Hills area. Dr. Rempel and a technician accompanied me on an expedition.

It had to be done in the early summer, when adult female black widows build maternity webs inside abandoned gopher holes, which are the only protection the barren land offers against prairie downpours. They warm their egg sacs in the sun that penetrates the burrow entrance.

So there I was, investigating abandoned gopher holes on the open prairie, frequently forced to lie down for a while. For someone terrified of black widows, it's no fun to be flat out in a field dotted with suitable homes for the venomous mothers-to-be.

We were able to find only three specimens — two of them in another traditional habitat, under the seat of an outhouse, which is an excellent place for catching flies. (And, as a number of human males have found, an equally excellent place for a spider to mistakenly bite whatever might dangle into its web.) The outhouse that provided our pair of specimens was, of all places, in the local schoolyard. In the end, I had to send away to Texas for a supply of adult females, many of them already fertilized. Within weeks, I had a population of almost three thousand, most of them infants.

(Driving through Texas a few years later, I would occasionally stop to check out the culverts running under the highway. Every single one I looked into had at least one deadly female and her nursery web. Even later, when Tiff and I visited the Devil's Tower in Wyoming, I checked out the prairie dog colony at its foot. The first hole I looked into had its expected occupant, carefully turning the egg sacs suspended from her web to ensure thorough warming.)

For my Saskatoon research, then, with all those arachnid mouths to feed, I needed a constant supply of houseflies for the adults and tiny fruit flies for the young. I allotted part of my study grant towards hiring an assistant to oversee the raising of this livestock and the feeding of it to my spiders.

The person I found was an ebullient young woman named Jean Ryland, who was taking a break from teaching to do something "interesting." This job was certainly that.

Jean was very popular with all my friends. They used to gather in the lab, to relax and sometimes tease her. One day the mode of teasing was to try to discover which of all the forbidden words she most wanted to avoid hearing. Even I joined in. Just as we were all bombarding poor Jean with every dirty word we could bring ourselves to say in her presence, Dr. Rempel walked in.

I had known how affable he was — and how devout. (His brother was a bishop in the Mennonite Church.) That day, I discovered how wise he was. He simply smiled, said he was glad to see that all was going well and left. Nothing could have shut us up more quickly or more kindly.

My huge livestock collection was housed not in the Biology building but in its annex, in which a colleague was also raising and studying cockroaches. This was cause for a problem. The annex was headquarters for all campus activities related to home economics.

The dean, Dr. Hope Hunt, made regular nervous forays into our area. "What if your dreadful spiders get out? I won't have any kind of fly, and certainly not *cockroaches*, in my kitchens!"

Every month, she would remind us about the Farm Wives of Saskatchewan. This boisterous group of middle-aged ladies, filled with good humour and curiosity, would come storming into the building for their monthly meeting. Often, many came bustling into the lab, wanting to know what we kept in all those lovely jars.

I was terrified these ladies might unwittingly release one or more of my deadly black widows, so I decided to make the lab farm-wife-proof.

For this purpose, I contacted a Florida biological supply house to order an alligator: a live, three-foot alligator. By the time he arrived (dubbed Albert, in honour of Pogo's comic strip) I had fashioned a home for him — a five-foot wide galvanized tin pen, suitably waterproofed, with about a foot of water and some big rocks for basking. I also organized the food supply: live mice from the Department of Physiology in the Medical College.

On every Farm Wives Day, I tethered Albert in the doorway, where he appeared to be a stuffed doorstop until someone foolish enough to approach him saw his mouth open wide, out of which would come something between a roar and a hiss. Farm wives scattered in all directions.

Albert was remarkably effective as a deterrent to all unwanted visitors for the rest of my stay in the annex. When I achieved my Master's, I donated Albert to a local high school.

Throughout this time, I did not neglect my minor subject: Theatre.

Looking back, I am quite surprised, and occasionally amused, to remember just how much theatre I experienced during my undergraduate and graduate years.

It's difficult to understand today, given the widespread presence of professional theatre in Canada, but before the creation of the Stratford Festival in 1953 there was hardly any professional theatre right across the country.

My very first experiences with the stage came with Regina's annual summer exhibition. Two years in a row, the midway featured performances by two icons of a certain kind of theatre.

First, there was the fan dancer, Sally Rand. Although she gave the impression of modest nudity, I suspect she wore a body stocking. Certainly, her manipulation of two gigantic feathered fans was accomplished and elegant. My grandmother thought she was "splendid." And Sally abided by the law: at the end of each performance, when she held both fans aloft, she froze. Total nudity, it seemed, could not be accompanied by movement of any kind.

The second icon was the legendary stripper, Gypsy Rose Lee. She was delightful in quite another way — and equally lauded by my grandmother. For her big number, she came onto the stage in a voluminous and elaborate costume, flanked by a bevy of semi-nude beauties. To the accompaniment of Miss Lee's wry comments, she used bits and pieces of her own costume to completely clothe her entire chorus. Wonderful!

Less wonderful were the offerings of our own amateur group, the Regina Little Theatre (aptly named!). Their offerings included unsuccessful attempts by local media celebrities to achieve elegance and sophistication in such Noel Coward works as *Private Lives*. (I was later to develop some sympathy for these actors when, in summer stock in 1960, I was cast in the same play.)

MY OWN THEATRE CAREER BEGAN IN public school. My very first performance was given when I was about twelve, in a one-man show that was, in a sense, both prophetic and hypocritical. I can remember only its title: *Why I Am a Bachelor*.

My second performance was still in public school, a simple little fairy tale, *The Princess and the Woodcutter*. (Tiff once asked, facetiously, which role did I play?) I remember very little about it, except for one minor incident during rehearsals. My leading lady, impressed with my reading of some particular line, tried to observe that, as an actor, I was unlike any other. "You're ... you're ... oh, what's the word ...?"

"Unique?" I offered, modestly.

"That's it!" she said. "That's it, exactly." Then, loudly, to the rest of the cast, "That's what he is! Unique!" She apparently enjoyed using the word and laughed uproariously. The only problem was that she pronounced it as if it were spelled E-U-N-U-C-H.

I can't resist this probably apocryphal story about Vice President Dan Quayle. One day, travelling with his team of assistants and bodyguards, he stopped for lunch. At the chosen restaurant, he glanced at the menu and then looked up at a rather buxom waitress to say: "I think I'd like a quickie." One of the secret service chaps leaned over and quietly observed, "Mr. Vice President — I believe it's pronounced 'keesh.'"

(This is not apocryphal: Tiff and I were briefly in Washington, DC around when Quayle was vice president, and saw a street vendor offering t-shirts bearing the image of Munch's famous painting, *The Scream*, under which was printed: "DAN QUAYLE FOR PRESIDENT????")

I still have the small silver cup I won for my performance in a Chekhov one-act play usually known as *The Bear*, but, in Saskatoon, it was called *The Boor*. My final performance at university was in Christopher Fry's *A Phoenix Too Frequent*, a romantic comedy in verse; but, as I remember in this production, something of a farce.

I was playing the role of the Roman soldier, Tegeus. Opposite me, as the lovely Dynamene, was a girl named Margaret West, from Regina. Interestingly enough, we were both working on Master's degrees in biology — me in spider muscles and she in the muddy odour in fish (a problem at the time for the province's fishery industry. It made me think of my childhood spearing of buffalo fish in the shallows in front of our cottage and the muddy horror of their taste).

Each of us was a bit leery of the other's subject and its implications. For me: had those hands I clutched so romantically just been dabbling in odiferous dead fish? For her: what might suddenly crawl out of my Roman soldier's tunic (as she shared with me a phobia about spiders)?

Aspects of my get-up for the play were problematic; I wore a red skirted tunic, so inexpertly crafted that its hem swooped and dipped drastically. This was covered with silver-painted body armour, formed of fibreglass, modeled on a much bulkier build than mine. This gave me the profile of a pouter pigeon. Then, there was my makeup — for face, arms and legs. Various techniques were tried during the play's run. On the first night, before the curtain went up, I stood in my dressing room while three students brushed on icy tempera paint that tickled as it was applied — and cracked as it dried, during the performance. I seemed to have been fashioned from aged mahogany. The next trial involved a dark reddish brown grease paint, slathered on and then covered up with lavish applications of powder. The powder made me sneeze, and the paint kept rubbing off onto

Dynamene's costume until she appeared to have been mortally wounded by our lovemaking. Finally, the three students resorted to spray paint, which coloured not only me but also my costume, my armour and anyone foolish enough to come within five feet of the procedure.

While I was still busy working out the musculature of the black widow spider, I joined a local amateur theatre group in Saskatoon, the Community Players. It was headed by a somewhat headstrong woman named Louise Olson, whose daughter, Beverley, was one of my fellow students at the university. Beverley became an excellent researcher, and supplied invaluable information used by Tiff in his novels — by then, married and divorced, she would be Beverley Roberts.

I shudder when I look at some of the production photos. I played the title role in *The Remarkable Mr. Pennypacker* — a play about a man who maintained two wives and two large families of children, each in a different city. Clifton Webb did a splendid job of the role in the film version. I, on the other hand, managed to look even younger than my twenty-three years and was thus ridiculous in the role.

The only good things about my experience were the children who played the two families, and the actress who played one of my wives. Her name was Norma Moore; she and her husband, John, would become lifelong friends.

I bombasted my way through bad accents to play in English farces. I worked backstage, doing dreadful makeup on other players and was hopeless at keeping track of props.

There was, however, one bright moment. I was asked to direct and design a production of *The Rainmaker*, the story of a charming charlatan whose one redeeming feature was that he managed to convince a very plain girl that she was truly beautiful. (Norma wanted to play the role, but her husband and I finally convinced her of an unavoidable truth: there was no way on earth to make Norma Moore look anything but beautiful.)

Then, disaster struck. The student playing the title role decided that he couldn't spare the time away from his books. It was too late to bring in anyone cold. The obvious but difficult decision was that I take over the role myself.

My life became a maelstrom of directing, playing, designing and, in fact, helping to fashion many of the design elements. The set's success would depend on scrims of various colours — so that, under different lightings, the audience could see beyond a ranch interior to the New Mexico desert and the hills that lay beyond it. The only scrims we could afford turned out to be seemingly endless bales of cheesecloth, laboriously dyed in my laundry room by Norma and John and me.

Despite a couple of foolish architectural mistakes in the design of the set, the whole thing came together in a very satisfactory way. The brief run was sold out — with people standing at the back every night. I crept out myself before the closing performance, to stand behind them and witness for myself how the scrims, the lighting and the music worked as the curtain went up. There are still a few old friends from those Saskatoon days whom I run into and who rave about the production.

At last, I had had a theatrical experience to be proud of. Its timing was crucial.

Shortly after *The Rainmaker*, I finished my black widow research. And then I finished writing my thesis, which was accepted and published. What did my thesis prove? That in the adult female black widow spider, there are 537 muscles, while in the tiny male, there are only 533. (Feminists, take note!) I was fortunate enough to be awarded a National Research Council fellowship that would support my working towards a Ph.D. in Biology at Yale, which had a strong entomological department.

There was just one problem. Doubt.

Did I really want to spend my life in scientific research? It could be tedious and it seemed to involve a lot of killing. I think that if Canada had had a flourishing theatre scene in those days, I would have sacrificed all those years of study and research and headed for the stage. But what stage? There was Stratford. Apart from that, there were hardly any active in the whole country.

Fortunately, I had three years during which I could take up the NRC fellowship, so I set up two possibilities for employment in the meantime to gain both an income and more scientific experience. As mentioned earlier, I applied to the British Colonial Service for a research post in what is now Ghana; but, in order to provide a more immediate base, I also applied for a job at the University of Saskatchewan in the Department of Anatomy. That application was accepted.

Most of my energies at the university were directed at taking over a research project investigating cancer in mice. The research had been started by a young medical graduate who had been seeking an additional degree — a Ph.D. Lack of money and the unexpected pregnancy of his wife had forced him to abandon the project, in order to start generating an income as a practising physician. So much time, effort and funding had gone into the project, however, that the head of the Department of Anatomy — Dr. Rudolph Altschul — was reluctant to abandon it. He hired me to take it over and to fill in whatever time I had to spare with other lesser projects, most of them describable as on-the-job-training.

The project was an investigation into how cancer rates in young mice might be affected if their mother had experienced a certain amount of oxygen deprivation at a known sensitive point of pregnancy.

Fortunately (at least from a scientist's point of view), several strains of laboratory mice had been developed in which the incidence of various cancers was quite predictable. In one strain, eighty per cent of the offspring would develop lung cancer. In another, one hundred per cent of the young would die of leukemia. And so on.

Pregnant females were subjected, on the ninth day of their pregnancy (a particularly crucial day in the embryonic development of mice) to five hours in an airtight container from which a controlled amount of air had been pumped out. In effect, it gave the animals only as much oxygen as they would receive if they were on the summit of Mt. Everest. Once the offspring of these mice reached a certain age, they were killed and examined to see if they had more or fewer tumours than would be expected in their particular strain.

Enter Bill Whitehead.

The experiment I took over had several hundred mice of each cancer-ridden strain. Every female had been given an identifying number. To my horror, this was done by using a scalpel to cut off a certain number of toes from each foot. Reading the remaining numbers of toes on each foot (front left foot first, rear right foot last) provided a lot of four-digit identification numbers.

I was assigned two assistants who fed the animals, cleaned

out their cages and examined the females every morning for signs of mating. In mice, this meant looking for a semen plug in the vagina. Almost all matings resulted in pregnancy. The mating date was noted and the female underwent oxygen deprivation nine days later. Ultimately her offspring would be checked for cancer.

By the time I took over, the whole process was well underway. This meant that most days I would spend from eight o'clock in the morning until eight o'clock at night with a stack of mouse-filled cages on my left, another stack of empty cages on my right and, in front of me, just beyond my dissecting space, a growing pile of mouse corpses, with every identification number and type of cancer carefully recorded.

Death resulted in much the same way as it would in a hanging. I would grasp the mouse's head in one hand, the tail in the other, and then jerk my hands apart, thus breaking the spinal cord.

Of course, in the science world, it is not said that the mice were "executed." They were "sacrificed."

I hated going up to the top floor, where the experimental species were housed. In one room, a collection of cages contained pathetic cats, deliberately brain-damaged in studies of cerebral activities; in another, several dozen dogs. The hall outside was filled with frantic barking or with loud music, which tended to pacify the dogs.

In yet another room, there were white rabbits with hardened arteries and rats with sewn-up incisions that could be anywhere on their white-haired bodies.

Then there was the mouse room. Banks of cages, filled with hundreds of little creatures, rustling and squeaking. Occasionally I would visit them, perhaps even eat my lunch with them.

It was a bit unnerving, however, when all that mouse noise suddenly stopped, and all those mouse eyes focused on my sandwich.

Two things happened when the experiment was finally completed and its results could receive statistical analysis.

I went over to the Mathematics Department to consult with one of their statisticians, who showed me how to do the appropriate assessment of my results.

I was horrified by his opening words.

"So — what results would you like to see?"

"What do you mean?"

"Just that. Depending on which analysis we choose, you can probably have any result you want."

All that killing for this.

I didn't select either a result or an analysis. I simply left the figures with him and went back to my own department.

Eventually we published a paper, which showed that in one strain of the mice, prenatal anoxia (oxygen shortage) reduced the incidence of cancer in male mice to zero.

To this day, I have no idea just how true or how significant that result might be.

The second thing, which I found out later, concerned the sense of humour among scientists. I went to a scientific congress held in Banff, where I read part of my paper detailing the experiment. Given the antics that went on in the dormitory, I decided that mature scientists didn't necessarily have mature senses of humour. They liked juvenile tricks, such as "apple pie beds" and pails of water balanced on partly open doors. I was encouraged to try a corny joke during the reading of my paper.

I described how the experiment had placed pregnant females

under conditions that approximated those at an altitude of thirty thousand feet — noting, with an expectant smile, that this was the reverse of the usual situation in our own society, in which we get the female high before we get her pregnant.

Nothing. Not a murmur. Not even a smile.

At that time, I was having more serious concerns: a growing sense of doubt about the academic path I had chosen. My mind understood this necessary cost of gaining vital (or even just useful) scientific knowledge, but my heart was troubled that, in only a few years of research, I had slaughtered thousands of spiders, insects and mammals.

There had also been the dozens of frogs I had paralyzed in the undergraduate biology labs I supervised, so that the students could observe the workings of the viscera of a living amphibian. The technique involved using a sturdy probe to stab each animal just behind its eyes, then, changing the angle of attack, forcing the probe down the spinal column to destroy the spinal cord. This was called "pithing the frog." I sometimes tried, feebly, to lighten this grisly moment by announcing to the class that the frog was now "pithed to the eyeballs."

In my spare time in the Department of Anatomy, I was sometimes asked to help the support staff set up "lab material" for the medical students. "Lab material" was the euphemism for human cadavers, which were stored in tanks of preservative liquid in a huge basement vault. My first encounter with the "material" remains unforgettable.

Every corpse was encased in a coating of brilliant yellow latex. And, since several researchers were involved in culturing various human and animal cultures, one of my regular tasks was to whip over to the University Hospital's maternity ward and pick up the raw material from which the nutritive medium of the culturing could be fashioned. The "material" was the human placenta. It had to be as fresh as possible, so this often meant getting to the obstetric theatre early and — from the observation deck — watching the birth process.

Occasionally, I would recognize the mother as a fellow student or a friend, but deemed it appropriate never to mention what I had witnessed.

WHAT WAS TO CHANGE THE COURSE of my life was something that happened in Ontario in 1953: the opening of the Stratford Shakespearean Festival. At first I was unimpressed: one theatre doing two plays a summer? What difference was that going to make? What I did not know was that there was a project to give Stratford actors work in the rest of the year, a touring company called Canadian Players that toured the country in a bus, with actors, costumes, sets and lights. They would perform one play by Shakespeare and one by Shaw, and they would visit dozens of Canadian cities and towns, wherever there was a stage — be it in a theatre, a school auditorium, or a church hall.

While I was hard at work in the Anatomy Department, the Canadian Players paid their first visit to Saskatoon.

Since I had never seen professional actors at work, I decided to see each show – *Macbeth* and *St. Joan*, each starring Douglas Campbell and Frances Hyland. I had never met either of them, even though Frances Hyland and I had attended the same high school (she was a couple years ahead of me).

I cannot describe the effect those two productions had on me; all I can say is that what I had dabbled in over the years had not really been theatre. This was theatre! I was hungry to be a part of it.

After the first show — *Macbeth* — I ran around to the stage door and asked who was in charge. The company manager, I was told. I asked to see him, and he was very helpful — a young man named Barry Dimock. He told me that in artistic terms, one of the actors was the leader, Douglas Campbell. Could I meet him? We'll see. A few minutes later, I was taken to his dressing room.

I can't remember much about that encounter; I was too exhilarated. All I can recall is the moment at which I stammered out: "M-M-Mr. C-C-Campbell ... huh ... huh ... how do you get to do this?"

His answer was brief and to the point.

"You leave Saskatchewan."

So, just before Easter in 1957 I resigned my post at the university and stepped onto a bus headed for Toronto.

One year later, I was working as an actor at the Stratford Festival, in a play directed by Douglas Campbell.

I DID NOT ARRIVE IN TORONTO unprepared to stay there. Before leaving, I had asked for advice from two people. One was the head of the university Drama Department, Emrys Jones, who had just returned from a year's sabbatical, during which he had produced radio drama for CBC Winnipeg. Jones offered to give me a letter of introduction to one of his actors, Arch McDonnell, who had since moved to Toronto and was busy working with CBC Radio.

My second advisor was my mother, who had lived in Toronto shortly before I was born. Her advice? Find a place to live that was both pleasant and cheap. Marje Thomson's suggestion did not take into account how much Toronto might have changed in over twenty years. "Look in the Jarvis Street area. It's a lovely spot, with boulevards and parks."

Regina's Library had copies of the *Toronto Star*; among the accommodation ads, I found a private hotel that was just a block from Jarvis and Dundas. It was more than affordable, and being just a block from Jarvis and Dundas meant that it was right in the middle of what had become the drug and prostitution section of the city. Not what my mother would have called a "lovely spot." My nightly entertainment was to huddle, a little nervously, behind the front window of my room and watch the police break up knife fights on the street.

I was certainly not the only innocent to come from the prairies to "Toronto the Good." I would later meet a pleasant woman, Heather Moller, who was hired by the University of Western Ontario in London to raise funds to support a scholarship that bore Tiff's name. She had grown up in a small town northeast of Regina, and when she first arrived in the big city, she boarded a Toronto Transit Commission bus with a five-dollar bill and offered it to the driver. He was dismissive: "Don't you know you got to have the right change? We don't deal with bills!"

Heather replied, apologetically, that she didn't know, and further explained that she had never been on a bus before.

"Never been on a bus! Say — where you from?"

"Saskatchewan."

The driver slumped in his seat, closed his eyes and gave up. "Just go sit down."

On my second night in Toronto I went off to the Crest Theatre to see a production of *She Stoops to Conquer*. The cast included Frances Hyland, Amelia Hall, Douglas Rain and Norma Renault — all of whom I would one day work with. It was splendid!

My other gloriously cheap nightly entertainment was to put on my elegant grey plastic raincoat, chestnut-coloured corduroy cap and cream-coloured gloves, and to go for a walk. I walked up Jarvis to Bloor Street, then all the way west to Jane Street and back again, a matter of some miles.

Days were spent in whatever activity might lead to work in theatre. There were the CBC Radio Drama auditions, which seemed to go splendidly. I was delighted when I was told I had passed, until one of my fellow auditioners told me that almost every well-known actor on CBC Radio had failed this first attempt.

Things went a bit better when I sought out Emrys Jones' friend Arch McDonnell. He and his girlfriend, Celia Sutton, the designer, were extremely kind and generous; they helped me get to know the city and occasionally drove me to the Muskoka Lakes area, where they ran a summer lodge which housed some of the actors working in Port Carling's summer theatre.

There were some troubling facts. The only professional theatre in the city — the Crest — would shortly close for the summer, and the handful of summer stock companies in the area already had all the people they needed. The small amount of money I had brought with me was relentlessly seeping away. The only other friend I had in the East was Jean Howard, now Jean Cole, my friend from kindergarten days who now lived in Ottawa. She would send me care packages: boxes of powdered milk, bottles of Cheese Whiz, packages of crackers. I would make it all last as long as I could.

Eventually, I got down to seventy-five cents, with only two weeks of paid rent left. I looked at the coins. There was a little more than enough to buy a hamburger and a chocolate milk-shake. Or I could go to a movie matinee. I opted for the movie, which turned out to be one of the loveliest and saddest I had ever seen: Fellini's *La Strada*.

I emerged from the theatre, tearful and utterly depressed. I made my way back to my hotel, where to my complete sur-prise I found a telephone message. A number and the words: *Call Mr. Young*. I didn't know any Mr. Young, but next morning I called the number. It wasn't "Young." It was "Ljungh."

Esse Ljungh — Head of Radio Drama for the CBC.

Mr. Ljungh's script assistant told me that I had been cast in his next drama. Was I available? I managed to indicate that I was. I was given the date, time and place of the rehearsals and the recording. Just in time, I was going to earn a bit of money as a professional actor.

The play was set in ancient Rome, and centred on the patron saint of actors, St. Genesius — who was played, appropriately, by one of the greatest radio actors this country has ever seen: John Drainie. Equally appropriately, it turned out, I played a classical fool — loudly, melodramatically and badly. I thought I'd never be asked to work again.

But I got another call — this time from a man named Henry Comor. He had apparently been a silent witness of the CBC Radio Drama auditions, and had just suffered the loss of his apprentice at the Peterborough Summer Theatre. Was I free for the next two months or so?

It was a wonderful summer. I shared a room and a hot plate with another apprentice, from Alberta. I got to play in all eight productions — and even received a good review from Robertson Davies, who was then editor of the *Peterborough Examiner*. Most of the actors, including Comor and his wife, Edythe French, were from England; they were well trained and effective. Others included Tom Kneebone and Larry Beattie, then a couple, and Mary Savidge (later known as Mary Savage) who would marry an actor I would work with and befriend later, Joseph Shaw.

As happens in theatre, each job seemed to lead to the next one — which, in this case, was to tour Ontario schools with the Earle Grey Shakespearean Company. As I would later discover, almost every actor I got to know would admit to having done some early learning with Earle Grey, including Timothy Findley.

Indeed, it offered a learning experience — although it was more a case of learning what not to do. Mr. Grey and his wife and leading lady, Mary Godwin, were then in their seventies, which meant among other things that their acting style was, to put it mildly, old school — in other words, a bit shaky and definitely melodramatic. Despite her age, Mary still insisted on playing all the Shakespearean ingénue roles and would not allow Mr. Grey to hire any actress younger than she. In our selected scenes from *As You Like It*, Mary's Rosalind was portly and stiff. So physically stiff, that is, that in the final scene, as she sank into a deep curtsey, we had to lower the curtain while two members of the company rushed forward to heave Rosalind to her feet for the curtain call. Even worse, her Orlando was a camp little fellow from Northern England. Most of his lines seemed to demand the addition of a "so there!" delivered petulantly, with hand on hip.

In the scenes from *Julius Caesar*, Mr. Grey played Cassius in a ragged red wig that had seen better days. Another of the Brits in the company observed that he looked just like Zena Dare in drag. I was not familiar with Zena Dare, but I think I got the picture.

We travelled around in an old bus, with Mary Godwin ensconced in one of the front seats next to a window she insisted on keeping open. I think she hoped that the chilly autumn air might firm up her jowls.

The only other actress was of about the same age; sweet and usually a little boozy. I will never forget her Boy Lucius in *Caesar* — wild-eyed and unsteady in wrinkled tights.

I remember playing Casca in a sweaty-smelling toga with a painted red border that kept flaking off. I also played some rather grand character in *As You Like It*, for which I was got up to look a lot like Bette Davis barging around as Elizabeth I — lots of heavy velvet and ruffles.

I was quite happy to see the tour end.

THE REST OF THAT WINTER BROUGHT a bit of television work and a couple of industrial shows. The latter were very welcome. They were tours of skits and musical numbers, which were put together to act as commercials for whatever company staged the tour. They paid extraordinarily well.

In one of these industrial shows, the company included a name well known to Toronto audiences, the veteran actor Joe Austin, and a singer who later become much better known, Igors Gavin. The sponsor was Imperial Oil. In one of my sketches with Joe, he was delighted that I played his psychiatrist crazier than the dazed patient he portrayed. He also complimented me on my timing, which pleased me greatly.

("Ask me what the secret is of great acting."

"Okay, what is the —"

"TIMING!")

In the spring, I auditioned for Stratford and was invited to join the 1958 company. There was, however, a problem: a sudden call from Actors' Equity, which I had just joined. I was told that I must change my name. There was already a William Whitehead in American Equity, with which we were then affiliated. I had to come up with a new name that very day, because the Stratford programmes were about to go to press. After much agonizing and many rejected choices, I decided simply to use my two Christian names, with a slight spelling change in the second one. Thus, for the next four or five years, I was known as William Fredric — and, to some close friends, Bilfred.

(How I wish someone had thought to tell me that all I had to do was insert a middle initial into my name!)

I arrived in Stratford by bus and was amused by the signs I saw as we drove in along the main street. First came a huge sign bearing the single word "FAG." I turned to another company member sitting beside me, and before I could ask he told me that it was the name of a German-based factory that produced parts for heavy machinery.

The next sign I saw was similarly startling: STAN BLOWES FOR FESTIVAL TICKETS. Again, my companion explained. It was not someone named Stan, so eager for Festival tickets that he would do practically anything to get his hands on them. No; it was the name of a local stationer who sold Festival tickets. (I

later discovered I was distantly related to him. If you can follow
the complications: his wife was the sister of my grandfather's
sister-in-law — my Great Aunt Minnie, who was married to
Grandad's brother, Walter.)

I still have cherished memories of each of the small roles I
played that summer. In *Henry IV, Part One* I was the British
soldier who flourished the Royal Banner in all the battle scenes.
The damned thing seemed about twenty feet long, and was
attached to something I first thought was a refurbished hydro
pole. Flourish? They had to be kidding!

In this case, "they" was the director, Michael Langham. He
would kindly excuse me from observing the other scenes so I
could go out into the baseball field north of the theatre and
practise "flourishing." I began to get the knack of it. The next
time we went through a battle scene, the flag — I thought —
behaved magnificently. In the scene's final moments I gave it
what I thought was a particularly grand swirl.

Michael's wry comment: "Bill, there are six people in the
second row who are absolutely furious ..." I knew there were
no people at all that day, but turned to look. There was my
banner, draped, covering six seats.

I also played an acolyte in the opening scene, which Michael
had borrowed from another play. It was the cathedral funeral
of Richard II; I was the one with the censer. The action of
the scene included something so violently terrifying that the
choirboys and acolytes were supposed to run away or collapse
and hide their faces in the Bishop's robes. I was among the latter
group. We were to stay like that for quite a while. Later in the
summer, during an actual performance, the audience began to
suffer growing paroxysms of coughing at exactly that point,

while I was hiding my face. When I looked up, all I could see was smoke. It was coming from my censer. The props people had put in far too much incense. All I could do was quickly follow my fellow choirboys and acolytes who had run offstage, and, later, apologize to the company for the disruption in which I had unwittingly participated, even if I didn't actually cause it.

The only lines I got to speak that summer were as a messenger in *Henry IV*. I lurked in the dark area under the audience and, on cue, pelted up the sloping ramp (called, to my amusement, the vomitory) and dashed onto the stage, breathless and just able to force the words out.

Our vocal coach that year was from England: Gwyneth Thorburn, of the Central School of Speech and Drama. I didn't know it at the time, but she had taught Tiff when he was sent to England after the Festival's first year. Nor did I know that one of our stars, Eileen Herlie, had toured for many months with Tiff in a British production of *The Matchmaker* by Thornton Wilder.

It was Gwyneth who solved my breathing problem. She taught me how to make an uphill entrance without exhaustion; I was to go through a wind-up procedure, swinging one arm in huge circles with as much energy and acceleration as possible, and then, instead of throwing an imaginary ball, throw myself up the ramp and onto the stage. It worked!

I didn't have much to do in *Much Ado About Nothing* — except admire the splendid Beatrice and Benedick of Eileen Herlie and Christopher Plummer. (I did have one bad moment during rehearsals, when I was watching from the audience. I was close enough to overhear Michael Langham and Christopher

Plummer, in a quiet moment, discussing a piece of business. Michael said: "Oh, I suppose not. You might look like a BF." I was appalled. Had Bill Fredric become the epitome of a fool? It was with great relief that I heard from one of the British members of the company that "BF" meant "bloody fool.")

Eileen's voice was extraordinarily lovely — including her singing voice, which I would ultimately hear, years later, when she sang the title song from a Broadway musical I attended, *Take Me Along*.

At Stratford, she realized early on that as good as the Festival Theatre's acoustics were, they required a slower delivery than most performers normally gave. Whenever the place was empty (although, sometimes, I secretly watched from the balcony), Eileen spent hours alone, speaking all of her lines until she was satisfied that she was speaking more slowly without sounding as if she were speaking slowly.

I can't imagine a better, wittier, more subtle Benedick than Christopher portrayed that summer.

Ever after, I was frequently delighted to be in a Stratford audience. One of the most memorable productions I saw — although far from the best — was Robin Phillips' *Antony and Cleopatra*. The casting of the female lead was stunning in the literal sense. Cleopatra was played by one of the loveliest, funniest comediennes in any theatre — Maggie Smith. Only a few minutes into the performance, there was the sharp sound of a seat hitting its own back. A figure in blinding white had leapt to her feet and was pounding up the steps of the aisle, heading furiously for the exit. It was Zoe Caldwell. I had seen her come in, and knew to what great acclaim she herself had played Cleopatra. Her unmistakeable voice was now plainly heard: "Oh … for Christ's sake!" Those words echoed in my own mind throughout the rest of the evening.

All I did in *Much Ado* was mime the role of a flautist up on the stage balcony. I had based my makeup — for whatever reason — on the current Governor General, Vincent Massey. Somehow, reporters got to know this and when the GG came for a visit, press coverage included a shot of the two of us.

Mr. Massey was very nice about the whole thing.

I didn't have much to do in *Winter's Tale* either, but I remember it best for two reasons. It was directed by Douglas Campbell, who had told me to get out of Saskatchewan if I wanted to work in theatre. And it included one of my first brushes with someone who would become truly famous.

Dougie wanted the rural scenes to be bumptious, rollicking and as rude as we liked. I was one of the shepherds. One of the company, John Gardiner, a good-looking young actor from Scotland, took this to heart. He bought a child's set of plasticine — different-coloured strips of the stuff — and set it out in the sun to get soft. Then he mashed them all together to form a monstrous, multicoloured phallus. He would smuggle it on stage under his tunic — partly to keep it warm — then, when the action got uproarious, he would sneak up to one of the shepherdesses and, from behind, thrust his "instrument" into her hand. The staging had me right beside one of them the night he did it to her. Her reaction was intense. The scene became the most uproarious of the season. In keeping with her screams of laughter, I reached over and reassuringly patted her swelling stomach. And that was as close as I ever got to meeting Amanda Plummer. The actress was Tammy Grimes, Christopher's pregnant wife.

As for John Gardiner, I was delighted to know that outside of the Festival season he roomed in Toronto with Barry Dimock, the young company manager of Canadian Players, who had arranged my Saskatoon meeting with Douglas Campbell.

I also remember John for his manner of telling jokes. This was one of them: In a somewhat stuffy club in London, a group of old duffers are sitting around, telling tales of their times in "Indjuh." When the subject of Indian tigers comes up, one launches into his own adventure with one of them: "It was when one of the great beasts was terrorizing the whole area — creeping into villages and killing ... oh, I don't know how many of the natives. So I decided to do something about it. I took me bearer and me gun out into the jungle, determined to find the bugger. Just as we entered a clearing, damned if he wasn't there — ten feet long if not longer — lashing that great tail. I signaled for me bearer to pass me the gun and just as I was aiming, damned if that monster didn't spring at me with the loudest roar I've ever heard: AAARRRGGGHHH!" (Pause to recover. Then continue quietly.) "I shit myself ..."

At that point, John stopped, laughing helplessly. And made no sign he had anything else to tell.

Now, I had heard the joke, and knew that John had failed to reach the punchlines, which were: One of his listeners piped up with, "Well, old boy — who's to blame you? I mean, with a great beast like that ..."

To which the hunter replied, dazed, "No. Not then. Just now. When I went 'AAARRRGGGHHH!'"

ODDLY ENOUGH, SOMETHING I GREATLY ENJOYED that summer were my hours as an unofficial volunteer in the Properties

Department. I had become friends with its head, the designer Brian Jackson, and soon found all my spare hours taken up with the magic of making various materials look as if they were something else entirely.

Fibreglass became metal armour. Felt, stiffened with glue and painted with black and silver, was transformed into wrought iron decorations for furniture and lamps.

With all those shepherds and shepherdesses in *Winter Tale*'s bucolic scenes, we needed a lot of wool, which was obtained from a sheep farm just out of town. It was contaminated with sheep manure and urine. One of my jobs was to clean it up. I laboured at it for days, finally showing my pristine wool to the designer, Tanya Moiseivitch. To my horror, she took one look and said, "Oh, Bill — it's far too clean. Can't you dirty it up a bit?" So I spent more days using brown and yellow paint to recreate the condition in which I had first found it. Such is the theatre.

That's when I met one of Brian's young assistants, Don Lewis. Years later, I would meet him again — as an actor. It was then that he told me of his experience with Actors' Equity and names. When he called to have his union category switched from prop maker to actor, the clerk to whom he spoke asked him to hold the line while he checked Equity's lists. When he came back on, he declared that Don Lewis could not join Equity as an actor because there was already a prop maker with that name. Don patiently explained, once again, that yes, Don Lewis had been a prop maker and that, indeed, that prop maker was him, but now he wanted to be listed as an actor. Nope. He couldn't remove his name from the lists and no name could be duplicated. And so, Don did a version of what I had done. He took his middle name and used it as a surname, becoming Lewis Gordon — a character actor who delighted Stratford audiences for years.

IT WAS GREAT TO WELCOME OLD friends as Festival visitors. My former schoolmate, Jean Cole, came from Ottawa with a friend to attend Duke Ellington's concert that summer. I took them to dinner at one of the town's few restaurants — the Chinese Golden Bamboo. We were invited to join a table that included Robert Goulet, who was starring in *The Three-penny Opera*. The group also included another singer from the cast — Alan Crowfoot, a vastly large chap who had had plenty to drink. He got into an argument with Goulet, stood up, and dumped a huge bowl of chop suey into the star's lap. Eventually, the excitement died down; the rest of the meal went well.

I WAS PARTICULARLY HAPPY WHEN, AT the end of the summer, I was invited to become part of the next tour of Canadian Players, even though I had no idea then just how beneficial it would prove to be.

What it did was provide me with two friendships that were among the most valued and important relationships of my entire life.

The friends? Marigold Charlesworth and Jean Roberts. They were a couple, and had come from the British theatre a year or so earlier, hoping to found a new theatre in Canada. At first they settled in Calgary, thinking that petroleum wealth might help them do just that. Later, it would. But not then. So they decided to try Ontario.

Marigold would play Juliet in Romeo and Juliet, while Jean — simply as a volunteer — worked tirelessly at the making of sets and properties. All I saw of Jean in those days was a pale, exhausted face, a paint-stained shirt and torn, baggy trousers.

The company's patroness was Lady Eaton. Towards the end of rehearsals, we were told that Her Ladyship wanted to offer us a farewell reception at her country estate near King City, north of Toronto. I had heard how vast it was. (I believe it is now a college.)

We all got cleaned up, dressed up, and bussed out to King City (I even bought a suit). When I entered the house, the first person I saw was Jeannie Roberts. I couldn't believe the transformation. A gorgeous silken print dress, silk stockings, high heels, beautiful make-up — with her auburn hair fashioned into a Dutch-boy bob.

Struck most of all by the hair — and reminded instantly of one of my favourite childhood stories, about the little Dutch boy who saved his country before water pressure could enlarge a hole he had found in one of sea walls — I blurted out something that I realized instantly was the wrong thing to say. But it was too late ... "My God, Jeannie. You look just like you should have your finger stuck in a dike!"

I'm extremely happy to say that Jean and I are still the best of friends.

One of my most vivid examples of the treachery of words.

I should also point out that it was Jean who first told me a story that ultimately would delight both Tiff and me. She swore it had actually happened:

After a British clergyman had visited Canada briefly, he was besieged with questions about Canada and Canadians.

Finally, he decided to present his answer from the pulpit. "I would ask you to imagine that the entire population of the world — men, women and children — once went walking along a great roadway. At one point, the road forked. Most of the vast assemblage chose the fork labelled THIS WAY TO HEAVEN. There was, however, a smaller group who chose the other route. These were the Canadians, and their sign proclaimed THIS WAY TO LECTURES ABOUT HEAVEN."

In later years, working with Jean at the National Arts Centre in Ottawa, I would join her in viewing certain Royal Commissions as just that — lectures about the desirable, without prompting any action to obtain it.

The Canadian Players tour featured *Romeo and Juliet* and *Pygmalion*. It lasted for eight months, stretching from St. John's to Victoria. In Newfoundland, one of their stages was in a basement auditorium used as a Catholic Church Hall. What we didn't know was that, above us, the ground floor housed a bowling alley.

That night, *Romeo and Juliet* unfolded in an endless thunderstorm.

Although neither of our productions was particularly brilliant, Newfoundland received us with typical and riotous welcomes — especially in the smaller centres.

We reached these by travelling on the "Newfie Bullet" — a narrow gauge railway that in summer would stop periodically if passengers wanted to pick blueberries. On this winter tour there were no unscheduled stops, but I swear that in every community in which we played, much of the citizenry would board the train with us and join in the carousing until we all reached the next town.

Following our Christmas break in Quebec City, I was asked to become the stage manager, filling a vacancy created by a misunderstanding over the tour's dates.

I was a good stage manager. Science had taught me to be thorough, resourceful and organized; it also made me capable of long hours of hard work. It was a great eight months.

The only problem with the new job was that I also had a role to play in *Romeo and Juliet* — the Duke, Escalus. So, every show I would throw on my costume, which involved an impossibly tall hat and a heavy velvet gown, shout out a few commands to the citizenry, then strip back down for action backstage. All of this worked quite well — until we hit the huge new auditoriums in Calgary and Edmonton. I can't remember which one of them had the problem, but there was a breakdown of communication lines between backstage and the lighting booth, high on the back wall. That meant I had to spend as much time as possible up in the booth, giving lighting cues. That also meant that the second I was stripped for action, I had to gallop through a basement maze of hallways and chambers, find the right staircase and pelt up it until I fell, breathless, into the booth.

On one of my gallopings, I took a wrong turn. Some community meeting was suddenly confronted with a wild-eyed madman in tights, t-shirt and full makeup. I screeched to a halt, shouted out "Sorry!" and dived back into the right passageway. I wonder what they thought.

A touring company becomes a family; this was a glorious time. We all did whatever we could to help everyone else. Whenever we reached a new town, one of us would go around making up a "bus shopping list" — and then go off to do whatever shopping was required. My seatmate was a delightfully slight actress named Debbie Cass, who was playing the Nurse in *Romeo* and Mrs. Eynsford-Hill in *Pygmalion*. She was good at doing the drugstore stuff, and was completely unflappable — even when she found herself saying such things as: "Six prophylactics, five packages of Ex-Lax and what do you have that's good for constipation?"

One of the highlights of the tour for me was a visit to Ganong's chocolate factory in St. Stephen, New Brunswick. They don't make Caramilk bars, but they do use a similar technique for getting hard chocolate to surround a syrupy interior. I'm pledged to secrecy; all I'll say is that the process mimics one of the processes in our own bodies.

At the Christmas break, we reassembled in Toronto. As our director, Tony Van Bridge, was playing at the Crest Theatre, we all trooped off to see him in *The Entertainer*. I was particularly taken with the performance of one of the younger actors whose work I had not seen before, although we had once been introduced after a chance encounter at Bloor and Yonge in Toronto. The actor's name was Timothy Findley.

Then, it was back on the road to finish the western leg of the tour.

We were a mixed lot — a relatively small group of native-born Canadians, well outnumbered by colleagues from Britain. It was wonderful, in the west, to watch this latter group encounter two of the extremes of the Canadian climate. We flew up into northern Manitoba, to the mining town of Lynn Lake. Few of the Brits had ever seen snow that deep or felt temperatures that low.

The locals took full advantage of the Brits' innocence. Two hunters had shot a wolf a few days before; they arranged the body in a standing position outside one of the buildings. They managed to convince (temporarily, at any rate) our newcomers that it had been so cold, the animal had been frozen stiff before it even had a chance to fall to the ground. Scepticism finally rescued them. The men among them were particularly impressed with a small crocheted item that the local ladies had for sale. It was a multicoloured tube of wool, known — at least, for the tourist trade — as a "peter heater." Another popular item was a kit for making buckskin moccasins. Its name was "Make-a-Moc." This elicited much posing and a take-off on one of the opening lines in *Romeo and Juliet*, "You bite your thumb at me, sir?" It soon became, offstage: "You make-a-moc of me, sir?"

By the time we reached Vancouver Island, we were at the other end of the climatic spectrum. The drive down the Malahat to Victoria is absolutely spectacular — lush, steamy Pacific rainforest, so primeval that I kept thinking: *if a dinosaur sticks its head out from those giant ferns, I won't be a bit surprised!* Our British colleagues were utterly astounded and enchanted that anyplace in Canada could look like this in the winter.

And by the time the tour ended, Marigold and Jean had finalized their plans for the coming summer, 1959. They would produce a season of stock at Ontario's venerable Red Barn Theatre at Jackson's Point, on the south shore of Lake Simcoe. And, along with most of the Canadian Players, I was invited to join them, which is why I offered only regrets when Stratford invited me back. Instead, for the two-month period before Red Barn rehearsals were to start, I joined a fellow Canadian Player, Herb Foster, in circumnavigating the United States.

We bought a used 1953 Monarch — a traditional first car, a red convertible — and set out. Across the northern states to the Pacific, down the west coast, back through Texan deserts to Florida, then up the east coast to visit friends in New York and Ottawa. Our final destination was Jackson's Point, north of Toronto, and the Red Barn. By the time we reached Toronto we were completely broke, exhausted and almost without belongings. Practically everything in the car had been stolen — bit by bit — as there was no effective way to lock a convertible.

Our most harrowing adventure came early on, as we crossed the northern states. By the time we reached Yellowstone National Park, our brakes had completely given out. In our automotive innocence, we had never tested the emergency brake. When we tried to park beside the rocky plateau that houses Old Faithful, we couldn't stop. We broke through one of the loops of iron chains that borders the parking lot and rolled merrily towards the geyser, which was then in full eruption. We managed to circle the great plume of steam and water. As we had begun to slow down, we hoped that the next chain would stop us completely. It did, but not until we had managed to break it as well.

The park officials were kind, sympathetic, and helpful — up to a point. Obviously, the car needed servicing, but so early in the season there were no mechanics up in the park who could help us. We had to descend into the valley in order to find an open garage in the next town.

Was the road going down as steep as it had appeared to be on the way up?

It was.

We were saved from total disaster by the snowbanks that lined the steep, narrow highway. Every time we began to accelerate to the point of losing control, I would steer the car over to the right so that the passenger's side would crunch along the snow and slow us down. This was a bit unnerving for the passenger, but it got us all the way down into the valley. It was the only part of the whole trip during which Herbie stopped talking. We were supposed to stop at the exit booth and check out, but all we could do was shrug and wave as we careened past it.

We made it to town and got the brakes repaired, and we made it all the way back. We were broke, but happy.

Within a week of returning to Ontario, we were both up in Jackson's Point, rehearsing Thornton Wilder's *The Skin of Our Teeth*, starring Toby Robbins.

When the season ended, we all returned to Toronto — where Herbie and I amicably went our separate ways. I began to accept roles at the Crest Theatre, which had taken Jean Roberts on as production manager.

As at the Red Barn, my roles were small, but they kept coming. One of the plays we did that season was *The Schoolmistress*, by Arthur W. Pinero. At one performance, we were to have a distinguished personage in the audience: Dame Edith Evans, who had played the title role early in her career. She was in Toronto to reprise her most famous role for CBC television — that of Lady Bracknell in *The Importance of Being Earnest*, by Oscar Wilde.

Dame Edith had agreed to give a poetry reading from the stage following the show. The management wondered: would she, at her age, feel more comfortable with a microphone — especially in such a long and narrow house as the Crest Theatre? But who was going to ask the possessor of one of the most famous voices in the English theatre if she required amplification of the sound of her words?

It was Jean, with her gentle, Scottish diplomacy, who made the offer. And here is the answer she received: "Oh, no, dear. Thank you, but no. You see, wherever I am, I simply discover someone sitting at the very back of the house and then I send out a silken thread to that patron, with the intention that he take hold of one end. Then, I carefully pull on my end until the thread is absolutely taut. If he does his job and I do mine the thread will remain taut until the end. And then I simply send out the pearls, one by one."

If Eileen Herlie had her way with words in the theatre, Dame Edith certainly had hers.

That whole season was an exciting time for me. At one point, in the evenings we were playing the Scottish play, while in the afternoons we were rehearsing *You Can't Take It with You*. Amelia Hall and I were in both; one day, on the way to rehearsal, Millie suffered a crime. Someone grabbed her purse and ran. God! The uproar! For a tiny person, Mill could certainly work up a storm. The police were summoned. We were all interrogated. It was splendid. The Big City. Theatre Stars. *Crime*.

On the way to my dressing room that evening, I passed Bill Needles' room. He was about to play MacDuff. He was putting cold cream on as a base for his makeup. He wasn't in *You Can't Take it with You*, so maybe I could be the one to tell him all about it!

"Bill! Bill! Did you hear about Millie this afternoon?"

"No, dear. What about Millie this afternoon?"

"Her snatch was pursed!"

He looked at me and give his Bill Needles grin.

"Probably been that way for years."

I have, as they say, dined out on that one a lot.

AFTER MONTHS, AND A COUPLE OF industrial shows and some radio and television work, it was summer again and time for the 1960 season at the Red Barn.

My roles got better and my colleagues better known — playing opposite Martha Henry in *The Moon is Blue*. (Good Lord! We were both in our twenties then!) I played alongside Carol Starkman (later Carol Rapp) in *Will Success Spoil Rock Hunter?* I also played alongside the popular Sammy Sales in *Harvey*. I had the lead in *Murder Without Crime*, which was stupidly melodramatic and not very effective. And, on the other end of the spectrum, I performed in *Private Lives* with Mary Savage and Joseph Shaw. I played Amanda's stuffy husband, Victor, and Marigold Charlesworth played Elyot's hopeless wife, Sybil.

At the end of the summer season, I returned to Toronto and the Crest Theatre. This time, I was cast in a terrific role in the British Second World War play, *The Long and the Short and the Tall*; I was the dour Scot named Macleish, and I used the accent of our Red Barn designer, Janet MacGregor-Smith, as the basis of my performance. Even Nathan Cohen, the notorious *Toronto Star* theatre critic, had a good word for me.

I was enjoying work in the theatre, but I was also beginning to wonder: is this how I want to spend the rest of my life?

Suddenly, I found myself working in the theatre in quite a different capacity.

This is how it happened. When Toronto's O'Keefe Centre opened, the box office sent out thousands of invitations offering season's subscriptions to theatregoers. It was not until hundreds of orders flooded in that they discovered that the box office alone couldn't handle them. A subscription department had to be created immediately.

Now, it happened that one of my friends in both the Canadian Players and the Red Barn was an actor named Alan Nunn. His wife, Marian, worked in the O'Keefe box office. It was she who suggested to the manager that her actor friends would be ideal to deal with demanding or irate subscribers; they would be tactful, pleasant and intelligent in handling mail orders and especially the flood of telephone calls from subscribers not pleased with their seat assignments. Most of them would have free hours during the day and, for those not currently employed on the stage, in the evenings.

And so, thanks to Alan and Marian, I joined most of my closest friends in working full time at the O'Keefe Centre. It was both pleasant and profitable.

It was during this time that I taught myself to silkscreen. At first, it was just a pastime. Then it became a small business. I produced greeting cards based on the costume designs of people I had come to know in the theatre — especially Brian Jackson, who had been running the Stratford properties room the summer I helped out there. Soon, I was silkscreening posters for the Crest Theatre and, when I decided to stay at the O'Keefe instead of going back to Jackson's Point in 1961, I also did all the Red Barn's posters — as well as occasionally travelling north to cook huge meals for the company.

My memories of the O'Keefe Centre include memory-photos of many of the great stars who came to Toronto for various kinds of appearances. Lena Horne — looking darker than she did in her films and even more beautiful. Harry Belafonte — who charmed the publicity and box office workers by bringing them huge boxes of chocolates, and, years later, charmed me. There were also three incredible female performers whom I had already seen elsewhere.

One was Marlene Dietrich, whom Herb Foster and I had seen in Las Vegas during our circumnavigation of the States. That first time, we were utterly enchanted by her ad libs. This second time, I discovered that they weren't spontaneous, but scripted — because they were all there, in Toronto.

Another was Ethel Merman, repeating the role I had seen in New York – Mama Rose in *Gypsy*. Then, it had been one of the most dynamic and effective performances I had ever seen. When I heard she was coming to Toronto, I urged all my friends to be sure and see her. Alas, most of the verve had been lost along the way. Her Rose was lacklustre, uncaring and dull.

Years later, I learned the reason. An unfortunate back condition had kept the star in constant pain for many months. My disappointment was replaced by continued admiration.

Then there was Judy Garland. I had seen her greatest show earlier, at Kleinhann's Music Hall in Buffalo, when she was so utterly "Judy" that at the end of the performance — during which I sat in the very last row of the orchestra — I suffered a brief loss of memory. At one moment, I was standing at the back, furiously applauding. The next thing I remember I was standing at the footlights, one of the crowd, yelling and jumping up and down with arms stretched up towards her. I felt just as wildly enthusiastic at the end of her Toronto performance.

Years later, during another of her Toronto appearances, I was invited to a Garland press conference. There, I was appalled at how gauche, unimaginative and trite the press could be.

"Who's your favourite male vocalist?" (Tony Bennett)

"Who's your favourite female vocalist?" (Peggy Lee)

"What's your favourite recipe?" (Shepherd's Pie)

When it came to my turn, I remained silent. I was too embarrassed. Perhaps my question would have seemed no better, but I wanted to know about her relationship with her hand-held microphone. She seemed to use it more as a prop — and as a stand-in for the one person she was singing to — than as an acoustic device. Any truth in that?

Then, the Crest Theatre was invited to revive its highly successful production of *The Long and the Short and the Tall* at one of New York's off-Broadway theatres — and I was asked to reprise my Macleish. To the great surprise of the Crest — and of many of my friends — I declined.

I had a very good reason.

Jean Roberts and Marigold Charlesworth had asked me to become a partner in a new venture: a three-month season of repertory theatre at the newly renovated Central Library Theatre at College and St. George Street in Toronto. Jean and Marigold would direct; Marigold would also act; I would run front of house and be business manager. It sounded wonderful, even though I had no idea just *how* wonderful it would be.

We started hiring actors in late 1961. Part of my job was to negotiate their contracts; it was a busy time. The longest negotiation — and certainly the most pleasant — was with Timothy Findley.

Actually, we wrapped up the contract fairly quickly. And then we just sat there, chatting. For hours.

Rehearsals began in January, 1962. Around the middle of February, by which time Tiff and I had become casual friends, he approached me with a problem. That evening there was to be a telecast of a CBC drama he had taped some months earlier — playing the title role in Jules Pfeiffer's *Crawling Arnold*.

The problem? His room had no television set.

Well, the story's pretty well-known by now. We arranged to meet, and then I realized that — having put most of my money into our theatre season — I was practically flat broke. My refrigerator was all but empty, and I could afford to stock it with only one of two sets of things — some cheese and crackers, or six beer.

It was Timothy Findley.

Yes.

So, when Tiff arrived, I confidently offered the beer, only to be told that he was on a drug called Antabuse and would become very ill if he had any alcohol.

We watched the show, and, as I have often told, for the next forty years, on a certain February date, I would turn and ask: "Tiffy — isn't it time you went home?"

"Home," when we first got together, was a small basement suite in a house near the intersection of Yonge and St. Clair. Soon, we had company. The Red Barn's designer, Janet McGregor-Smith, had a cat named McTavish who had recently given birth to kittens. She asked if we would consider taking one. No, we said. We would consider taking two of them. Given the long hours we would be spending at work, the pair would have each other's company.

The male was named Max (he was big) and the female, Mouse.

And thus was founded a feline dynasty that would accompany us to the end of Tiff's life.

When I was taken to meet Tiff's parents in their gracious Forest Hill flat, Allan and Margaret Findley greeted us warmly. After dinner, having coffee in the living room, Allan said, "Bill — there's something I want to show you, just down the hall. One of my paintings."

There was no painting — just a startling confidence.

"My son's queer, you know."

I could do nothing but nod slowly and finally say, "Yes, I believe he is."

I never told Tiff.

THE REPERTORY SEASON AT THE LIBRARY opened and was a great success. Tiff had roles in all three plays, including the male lead in *The Rivals*, the play that features the wonderful character of Mrs. Malaprop. She minces the English language by often not getting words and phrases totally right. "The pinnacle of perfection" comes out as "the pineapple of perfection." That kind of thing. In our production, the role was played by the delightful Cosette Lee. When the curtain came down on act one, Cosy burst into the wings in tears. "They're not laughing! I don't understand it! They're simply not laughing!" The stage manager explained. "Miss Lee, you've been correcting all the malapropisms. All of them."

For the rest of the evening, everything went well. The malapropisms were delightful, Tiff was at his most charming and the critical reaction would prove to be thoroughly enthusiastic.

Another play in the season was a daring choice for Toronto in the very early sixties: *The Balcony*, by Jean Genet. It was set in a brothel that offered more than just sex; it offered ordinary men the fulfilment of their wildest fantasies. Elaborate scenes were contrived: one man became The General — whose girl was costumed and behaved as his horse. Another became The Judge, who condemned his prisoner to be whipped by a giant, semi-naked executioner.

That was actually how the piece opened — in the dark, with loud whip-cracking and screams.

I remember one night, just after the curtain had gone up on *The Balcony*. As front of house, I was resplendent in a tuxedo, gathering up ticket stubs, when the doors across the lobby burst open. A young couple came galloping through, breathless after running up the three flights of stairs that led to our floor, and fell, heaving, into my arms.

"Have we missed the whipping?"

I almost regretted having to say, "I'm afraid so."

After all, doesn't the theatre do exactly what that brothel did? Sell fantasies?

The Genet piece elicited both protest and praise. And complications. Since there were several children in *The Rivals*, Toronto's Children's Aid Society insisted that two of their representatives be present, backstage, during every performance of *The Balcony* — just to make sure that the children were not being exposed to such filth, which included one piece of business Tiff had to include in his performance. He played a young revolutionary in an uprising that surged through the play's nation and, at one point, had to castrate himself onstage.

That moment was consistently carried off with great effect and without dangerous exposures. It did, however, create a few moments of confusion. One night, Tiff and I were going home on the subway, both deep in an appreciative reminiscence of that evening's performance. Out of the silence, I turned to Tiff and said, "I really liked your castration tonight." Tiff had just begun a grateful smile when we both noticed that people around us were staring at us with considerably mixed feelings.

A similar thing happened another night. We were talking about a party we'd been to the night before, hosted by Alan and Marian Nunn, two of our closest friends (Alan, like Tiff, was in all three of the shows). What was heard this time by those around us was: "God! The Nunns throw a great party! It's absolutely amazing how much they can drink without getting drunk!"

If only our eavesdroppers could have heard that extra "n."

THE SUBWAY WOULD BECOME ONE OF the main venues of misunderstandings for Tiff and me. One winter morning, having gone into Toronto on a commuter train, we were on our way to various appointments in the city. We started to discuss a problem we had at the farm. The problem involved a table-top birdfeeder we had placed outside the breakfast nook's bay window. The birds loved it, and so did our fifteen-or-so cats. It had become their favourite hunting ground. Our feline population once reached thirty-nine, which was when we adapted our brick woodshed into a winter retreat for the outdoor cats, complete with heat lamps, straw-filled nesting shelves on the walls and a cat-flap entrance.

With great diligence, we managed to persuade most of the hunters that the birdfeeder was out-of-bounds. But we had one failure: a cat called Mother, who had wandered in hugely preg-nant, and who continued to look pregnant even after delivering seven kittens. Mother had established a unique relationship with the birdfeeder. She didn't hunt there; she used the seeds' chaff as her litterbox.

Here's how our subway discussion ran:

ME: "Oh, Lord, Tiff — did you see? Mother shat in the bird
      feeder again this morning."

TIFF: "I know. Maybe it would help if we shut her up in the
      cat house until she learns to behave."

At that point, we became aware that morning papers all
around us were being lowered so that fellow passengers near us
could see just who these rude bumpkins might be.

THE THIRD COMPONENT OF OUR 1962 season at the Central
Library was an example of the British theatre of the absurd —
N.F. Simpson's *One Way Pendulum*. In it, an English family
of eccentrics goes through all kinds of vastly ridiculous and
fantastic attitudes and actions as if these absurdities were utterly
mundane. The son is teaching speak-your-weight machines to
sing the Hallelujah Chorus. The daughter is broken-hearted
because her arms aren't long enough to hang below her knees.
The mother, rather than hiring a cleaning lady, hires a wonderfully large Cockney char to come in and eat the leftovers. And
so on ...

As you might imagine, the comedy of the piece will only work
if the actors don't try to be funny, but simply live the action as
if it were the ordinary stuff of daily life. Strangely enough, when
we all tromped out, years later, to see a touring company do a
production, directed by the eminent Jonathan Miller, we were
astounded that he had chosen to have his cast play the comedy.
I think almost everyone was disappointed — including, we later
found out, some of the cast.

Tiff's role in *One Way Pendulum* was that of a defense
attorney in a trial held in a life-sized replica of the Old Bailey,

erected in the family living room by the father. At first, Tiff was terrified. He often had trouble learning his lines, and here he not only had to learn a lot of speeches involving complex legal issues and jargon, but was the one who had to introduce each new subject of interrogation in his cross-examinations. During rehearsals, however, he found his salvation. Since his character would seek each new line of questioning in the papers on his desk, Tiff simply used a torn-apart copy of the script as his papers; thus was he able to provide his own prompts.

The season went very well, and even made some money. Then, after a week's holiday at a Muskoka lake, we went to Jackson's Point to work for the summer at the Red Barn Theatre.

I stayed there, but Tiff was in one of the two companies, each alternating a week at Jackon's Point with a week at the Orillia Opera House to the north.

That summer we made a lasting friendship with a bubbly little actress, Judy Sinclair. She and Tiff played opposite each other in the romantic comedy *For Love or Money*. At the end of the first act, there is an amusing exchange between them involving the show's title. They have one of those so-called Broadway arguments about sex, climaxing in the girl loudly announcing: "I wouldn't sleep with you for love or money!" To which the guy replies: "Nonsense! You'd sleep with me at the drop of a hat!" And, after a few moments, a hat drifts down from above and floats to the floor. Curtain.

On opening night, however, it wasn't quite like that. (Another example of the treachery of words.) Judy dried. On the title of the play. There was an awkward pause. And then out came: "I ... I ... I wouldn't sleep with you ... not with you ... not for *anything!*" Tiff, who laboriously memorized his cues as well as his lines, was momentarily thrown. Finally, he managed to say: "Ridiculous! You'd sleep with me … like *that*!" And merely snapped his fingers instead of providing a cue for a desperate apprentice on a ladder, backstage. A few seconds later, cue or no cue, the apprentice released what he had been holding. And a hat floated mysteriously down to the floor. The curtain came down to somewhat puzzled applause.

It was a lovely season for Tiff. He was superb as Tom in *The Glass Menagerie*, and both powerful and funny as an overbearing, club-footed Mennonite patriarch in *Papa is All*. I heard that at one moment of cast tension during rehearsals, Judy managed to lighten the mood by putting on Tiff's prosthetic boot — which he'd removed to rest his foot for a few minutes — and stomped down to the front of the stage, singing an overblown version of "Somewhere Over the Rainbow."

Judy also appointed herself guardian of Tiff's stock of Antabuse, which he was still taking. Somewhere in his archives there is the envelope she used to set out for him each week, on which she'd written, in big block letters, "EEEAT YOUR PILLLLLS, YOU DDRUNGKENNNN FOOL!"

It was also a lovely season for me — and it was certainly lovely for our cats, Max and Mouse, who lived right at the Red Barn, with the apprentices feeding them the food we provided (although I suspect that both the Barn and its fields also provided many mice).

That summer season ended for me on a somewhat disturbing note.

On our very last night, up in Orillia, I became extremely and violently ill. The reason was simple: my old allergy to bananas. During the final meal at the Orillia boarding house, the cook served what appeared to be butterscotch brownies. They were absolutely delicious; I wolfed down several of them. But they weren't butterscotch brownies. They were banana brownies.

The banana effect did not hit me until much later that night, long after the final curtain came down and the closing party — at least for some of us — was over. We had, in fact, gone to bed, but I was awakened by an attack of nausea and rushed for the bathroom. The next thing I knew I was lying, semi-conscious, on the cold floor in a pool of vomit, moaning and choking.

Tiff was magnificent that night. He heard me, rescued me, cleaned me up and got me back into bed. By that time, my entire digestive system was wreaked with violent spasms. Without being too graphic about it, let me say simply that when I was lying on my side I could hit opposite walls with great shootings of various fluids.

It was dreadful. Tiff spent the entire night taking soiled linen down into the basement to be laundered.

We both survived, but from then on Tiff joined me in constant vigilance as we sought to keep me forever banana-free.

In retrospect, I believe that it was tension that exacerbated the banana effect that night. It wasn't just that the summer season had ended. For each of us, a career in the theatre was about to end.

It was Tiff who had brought the subject up in early August. An actor's life is filled with tension, uncertainty and a lot of very hard work. Perhaps in some other field he wouldn't need a drug that prevented any intake of alcohol. Perhaps he could actually become a social drinker. And — of much greater importance to him — perhaps he could become what he had reached for, sporadically, for years: a writer.

I was ambivalent about his suggestion. I had enjoyed my five years in the theatre, but I was also a realist. I was untrained. I had no spark of greatness as an actor, which Tiff did. Perhaps I could have continued to earn a living in the theatre; but, if I did, I wasn't sure how much satisfaction I would gain or be able to offer to employers. I relented. Together, we prepared for the next step.

The greatest challenge, for me, was to find out what that step would be.

Words and Pictures

*B*y the time our work was done at the Red Barn, we had just thirty dollars between us. (In those days, nobody got very rich working in the theatre.)

Fortunately, the Findleys owned a lovely little house in Richmond Hill, north of Toronto, and weren't ready to retire into it. It even had a swimming pool. Soon, Tiff got a job writing advertising copy for the local radio station, CFGM, which had just gone country-and-western. It was going to be a challenge for him, but he made it work. And in his spare time, he began work on his first novel, *The Last of the Crazy People*.

Meanwhile, I went down to Toronto, which meant a long trip involving two buses and a subway. I needed to see a CBC Radio producer for whom I'd worked as an actor. His name was Murray Edwards, and he had attended the University of Saskatchewan earlier than me. We had become friends, partly because I had rented a room in his Rosedale house before spending the summer of '58 in Stratford.

I was in luck. Murray had just been asked to produce a new educational series called *The Learning Stage* and he needed someone to take over the science stuff. The only problem was that work wouldn't start for another three months, and I needed work immediately.

He thought for a minute and then told me about a smaller project he had actually been avoiding, but which was still open to development. He described it and I thought it was as bizarre as Tiff's new job, but manageable.

And so, for thirty dollars a week, I spent the next three months with tapes produced by Voice of America, on which American scientists spoke unintelligibly (as far as non-scientists were concerned) about their most recent research. The tapes had originally been used by the US government as part of the attempt to break through the Iron Curtain, in the hopes of sharing information with Soviet scientists. The material had been bought at bargain rates by the CBC as cheap filler. My job was to edit the tapes, cutting out the most arcane bits, and to explain in simpler terms just what the hell they were all talking about.

But that wasn't the only time I was hired to interrupt someone. Later, on *The Learning Stage*, there was a terrific series called "The Face of Ontario." It was about little-known people, places and ways of doing things in the province — particularly in pioneer days. It was written and voiced by a charmingly garrulous gent, Miller Stewart. His voice — slightly high, slightly cracked and utterly folksy — was, to me, perfect for his material. To the producer, however, it could be grating. I was hired to interrupt him, to break his raspy flow from time to time with my own dulcet tones. He was both generous and gentlemanly about the whole thing. He would let me see each script in advance. I'd mark the interruptions to give him an idea of what I'd say — and away we'd go with the recording.

My favourite episode was one in which we went down to the marshes along the northern shore of Lake Erie to tape a show on swan migration. Just where the marshes met the lake, thousands of swans had gathered. Their massed honking and croaking would provide the background to the script we would later voice in the studio.

On that expedition, we carried with us a brand new CBC acquisition called a gunshot microphone. I think it was the first time it was put to use. It was about five feet long and highly sensitive. It could be aimed at a specific source of sound — such as someone in an audience, speaking out — and would isolate the speaker from most of the background sound. We planned to record part of Miller's script that way, on site.

Two things happened. Getting the damned thing to the site almost killed the sound crew. Packed in a huge, coffin-shaped crate with much padding, it was heavy. Carrying it through the swamp and the mosquito-filled air was sheer hell.

Then, it turned out to be so sensitive that it recorded something neither the producer nor I had heard until we got back into the studio to choose the best swan noise. Right in the middle of superb avian calls came Miller's marvellous, creaky voice, sounding very much like one of the swans: "I've got one of those cheap German bladders and have to take a pee. I'll be right back."

How I wish we could have used it!

I soon got Tiff taken onto *The Learning Stage* as a CBC broadcaster, thus releasing him from his country-and-western days. There would be an interview series with Canadian writers, Canadian composers and visiting theatre artists from abroad — including Alec Guinness, with whom Tiff had stayed in the early fifties while he was studying voice in London.

At one point, I bought some lumber and some tools and built Tiff an octagonal bench that would encircle a pear tree in the backyard. This, together with an old tilt-top drafting table that had been abandoned in Murray Edwards' basement, became Tiff's writing place. He was making progress with his novel and life was looking good — until the inevitable happened.

In time, Tiff and I had decided that he should stop taking Antabuse. We believed in both the value and the possibility of drinking wine for enjoyment, rather than as an addictive drug. For a while, that was how we lived.

One night, however, Tiff disappeared. It was Robbie Burns Day and the pipers had been parading all evening. Tiff, unknown to me, had followed one group down the street — and away.

When I couldn't find him, I was distraught, then appalled. Ashamed. The police appeared with a Timothy Findley I could barely recognize. Drunk. Dishevelled. Belligerent. He wasn't to be charged with disorderly conduct — only warned.

Was this what our future was to be like?

Well, yes and no. Yes, occasionally. But most of the time no.

Meanwhile, the first Findley novel was shaping up, and our work at *The Learning Stage* was being well received. My very first broadcast, in fact, won a prestigious Ohio Award. It was the first in a series of programs in which, each week, I would take an animal and come at it from eight different areas of study: biology, history, mythology, etymology, fiction, drama, industry, painting. Its title was "The Octagonal Approach to …" "Octagonal" because the series began with spiders, who have eight legs, and because of the eight areas of study. (Shades of my black widow days.)

Life was good, but there was one thing we both wanted to change.

As lovely as the Richmond Hill property was, we yearned to live right out in the countryside — and as much as we appreciated Tiff's parents' generosity, we wanted to own our own home.

That meant we needed enough money to buy a used car, to put a decent down payment on a property and to start paying off a mortgage. And so, in early 1965, we both got busy. Well, busier.

Even though his first book wasn't yet in print, Tiff started work on a second one. I took on the job of producing an entire summer radio series for Murray Edwards. I structured a number of series that would be introduced with short programs centred on the names for the days of the week — with each episode to be broadcast on its own day throughout the summer. I would write and voice the daily introductions, drawing on word derivations, mythology, history, etc.

Between the two of us we managed to buy a lovely little used Valiant — taking care to have all its brakes tested. Then, slowly, we saved up $3,000 — enough for a $2,000 down payment, with $1,000 left to cover whatever the property might most urgently need.

We first looked in the Caledon Hills area, northeast of Stratford. Lovely country, superb properties, but nothing under

$30,000 — not even a ramshackle little house whose open front door revealed a garbage-strewn room that looked as if it hadn't been occupied since Bonnie and Clyde had abandoned it in the thirties.

We switched our search to the countryside northeast of Toronto. We sought out realtors in Markham and Stouffville, describing to them our limited resources and our hopes of finding an old house on twenty-five or fifty acres — and definitely not in a suburb. We were repeatedly heartened by their responses: "Got just what you're looking for!"

Our optimism didn't last; certainly not after we had been taken several times to a modern bungalow in a suburban development. (Jimmie Durante might have responded to it with his favourite reaction to a plot twist: "What a revoltin' development this is!")

Finally, we just got in the car and went looking. And got lost.

We had no idea where we were when we saw a possible property on the lip of a lovely valley. Its FOR SALE sign bore the name of a female realtor in a town we had never heard of, Sunderland. We asked for directions at the next service station we encountered and managed to meet the realtor. We gave our usual spiel and were encouraged by her response: "Well, I've got a couple of places you might take a look at, and then we'll have a better idea of where to go from there."

We got into her car and drove up a highway and down a country road. She explained that there were two side-by-side properties for sale by the same family: one with over 350 acres, where the owner of both still lived, and one next to it with 50 acres — where his parents had lived until their deaths about five years before. It had stood empty since then.

We met the owner, a mild and wrinkled farmer named Nelson Purvis. We explained what we were looking for and asked if we could see the smaller place, which we then did. The house lay right beside the road, with a small barn-like building near it, and a larger barn in the near distance.

The house was really two houses made into one: an older frame building, with a newer brick addition through which we entered. The age descriptions were relative, we discovered. "Older" meant built in the 1840s; "newer" — the 1870s.

It was relatively clean and relatively intact, although there was a fair amount of sagging. When we stood in the living room and looked through its doorway to the door leading down into the basement, the top of one frame angled down to the left and the other to the right. Wallpapers peeled; paint showed scratches and chipping.

The houses were connected on two levels. When we went upstairs, we found five small bedrooms and one very small bathroom. Only one room was in bad shape, with holes in the walls that had apparently been chewed out by rats.

I was beginning to have my doubts, until we saw the gardens. They were filled with Victorian favourites: lilacs and mock-orange, peonies, delphiniums, hollyhocks, day lilies, lily-of-the-valley (as in Tiff's mother's bridal bouquet.) Even one of my grandmother's favourites bloomed here — scarlet lychnis.

Tiff and I looked at each other. Maybe. It would depend on the price. The realtor suggested we go back to talk to the owner.

On the way, I had a private word with Tiff: "Please. Leave the discussion to me. Don't say a word!" He promised, remembering, as I did, that when we had gone to a town near Richmond Hill to check out a piano that was for sale, Tiff had sat down, played a few bars and then exclaimed: "Oh. We've got to have it. I don't care what it costs." After which I sighed and tried to negotiate with the owner. And, since it was on Tiff's "must have" list, we bought it — to be picked up once we had a house in which to put it.

The realtor elected to stay in her car while Tiff and I hunkered down on the lawn next door to talk money with Nelson Purvis. His opening words were not encouraging. "Boys, I've got one price, and I've sworn not to sell until I get it."

Oh.

"It's $9,000. Take it or leave it."

I thought, *Tiff. Don't say a word.*

I managed to say aloud that we'd certainly think about it, and would let the realtor know our decision.

Somehow, though, we both knew what our final answer would be.

WITH A $2,000 DOWN PAYMENT AND a $7,000 mortgage, the deal was completed. This left us $1,000 to install the one major item the place was missing — a furnace. Once the move was accomplished, a mild and pleasant man named Doug Bursey brought his teenage son (and namesake) to install it. Doug Sr. would become the farm's first handyman; Doug Jr., the first of many part-time teenage gardeners.

For a variety of logistic reasons, occupancy began a week before any furniture arrived. (The bare essentials had been waiting at several used furniture outlets.) Nelson Purvis kindly offered the loan of two beds — one double, one cot. Three people would occupy them: Tiff and I and our Richmond Hill cleaning lady, Agnes Mortson, who would help us get the place ready.

Mrs. Mortson belonged in one of those *Reader's Digest* "Unforgettable Character" pieces. As a girl, she had been taken from Ontario by her family to a homestead southeast of Regina. This was in 1905, the year Saskatchewan became a province. She wore what Tiff called "Minnie Mouse shoes" and talked incessantly (and, to us, incomprehensibly) about her extended family, using only a bewildering conglomerate of Christian names. She peppered her accounts with mispronunciations and malapropisms.

"Oh, this room would make a perfect liberry!" and "Boys! We've got llama from Heaven!"

(On a walk into the back fields, she had discovered a large patch of huge, football-shaped mushrooms we knew as puff balls. That was the only year in all our time there that they appeared; they helped feed us for that first week. *Llama from Heaven.*)

We soon discovered more local linguistic oddities. Nora Joyce, who later became our housekeeper, would talk endlessly of her husband's suffering from "very close veins" and her own fear of memory loss from "old-timer's disease." In the nearby village of Cannington we met Libby, a lovely old woman who had the classic look of a witch. One of her former public school teachers told us of having taught her in grade four and, at the beginning of the fifth grade, of asking her class, "Where's Elizabeth?" One little girl had answered, "Please, Miss. She got married."

Libby's truncated education might explain her linguistic oddities — or perhaps she was a bit hard of hearing. She dropped first syllables from many of her words, telling us that her son worked for "Sumer's Gas" and holidayed in "Gonquin Park."

The local weekly paper, *The Cannington Gleaner*, also had its occasional linguistic oddities. Its "In Memoriam" column once contained a new version of a familiar couplet:

> Gentile Jesus, meek and mild,
> Bless the memory of this child.

The accidental conversion of "gentle" to "gentile" was, indeed, memorable.

I've already offered that paper's startling announcement about "oral sex education." In my own student days, of course, there was no need to ban formal sex education. It was simply unthinkable. What was banned in Saskatchewan high schools then was the teaching of the theory of evolution. Teachers were forbidden to mention it, and during school hours nobody could talk to students about it. That is why, on several occasions during my university days, I was invited to visit my old school after classes, where I would give a short lecture on this "dangerous, blasphemous" subject.

In Cannington, there was a happy candor and directness about our new friends and neighbours. The man who farmed the property across the road, Leonard Griffin, was small, feisty and loud — especially when he sang hymns at the top of his lungs, hymns he interrupted with loud "Hees" and "Haws" as he urged his team of beautiful black horses to get to work. One day, he surprised us by bringing along a visitor, the Liberal candidate in our federal riding. (We were an overwhelmingly Conservative stronghold.) As they walked up the drive — apparently unaware of our open windows — we heard the familiar booming voice: "Oh, yeah. A couple o' homos. Nice boys, though. Nice boys. You'll enjoy meeting 'em!"

Given how hard we were both working, and how often we had to be away from home, over the years we hired quite a few of the local teenagers to help us feed our animals and maintain the gardens. I think it was a credit both to our own integrity and to the open-mindedness of our neighbours that parents would compete to get their sons hired.

The only time we ever heard of concern over two homo-sexuals hiring teenage help involved one of Cannington's most memorable citizens. Her name was Jessie Nicholson, and she was the matriarch of a local hockey dynasty that included both Nicholsons and MacLeishes (her grandson, Rick MacLeish, was an NHL star then playing for the Philadelphia Flyers).

At one point, so we heard, Jessie was visited by her minister who verbally chastised her for allowing her grandsons to work for "those degenerates out on the eleventh concession."

That would be us.

And what did Jessie do?

She told her minister to go to hell and changed her church.

Heavenly woman!

The wages we paid were generous, but far from extreme. We encouraged each worker to establish a savings account and to keep it nourished.

What evolved, over the years, was a kind of finishing school for Cannington youth. We tried to fill in the gaps found in rural education. We began taking them to the theatre in Toronto and as far away as Stratford. When in Toronto, we would do casual courses in restaurant behaviour: how to decipher menus, handle tipping, deal with wine stewards, etc. We would take them shopping, helping them to find gifts for girlfriends or clothes for themselves. Above all, we would open our household library to them, which, given that its owners were professional writers, probably held more useful reference books than could be found in the local schools or the town's one-room library. And to the latter, we made regular donations of sets of reference books — some of the Time-Life series — in order to bolster local resources.

Many years later, well after Tiff's death, I made a special pilgrimage to Cannington. The occasion was the move (and enlargement) of the former library into the completely reno-vated and beautiful old town hall. The town hall once included a theatre on the second floor, where Tiff and I used to attend an Ontario version of *tableaux vivants*, presented by local ladies and gents in Victorian attire. With a suitable musical introduction and accompaniment (one well-pounded piano) the curtains would open on a living picture — the costumed citizenry, in frozen attitudes, depicting some period activity such as *The Tea Party* or *Lawn Bowling*. (The latter, in fact, was still a local recreation.)

After enough time to allow the audience to appreciate the intricacies of the scene, the curtains would close. After quite a lot of banging about, the curtains would eventually reopen to another musical fanfare and another setting. Charming!

And now I was back at this beautiful building to attend the official opening of the Timothy Findley Memorial Library. The event drew a huge and enthusiastic crowd and a plethora of speakers. My donation was Tiff's Mennonite roll-top desk, replete with all kinds of Findleyana that he used to keep in and on the piece, including copies of some of the books whose research or characters had local roots and a terrific photograph of Tiff with one of his favourite cats, Ezra.

When it was my turn to speak, I couldn't resist including two library fables that had greatly delighted us both.

In the first, a librarian one day is startled to see a chicken strutting towards her desk, uttering a staccato "Buk! Buk! Buk!" When the bird reached its destination, it raised one wing and commanded, "BUK!"

Somewhat mesmerized, the librarian took up one of the books on her desk and tucked it under the chicken's wing. The bird then wheeled around and marched out, muttering a contented series of "Buk ... buk ... buk ..."

This little scene was repeated twice. Finally the librarian, intrigued, decided to follow the chicken out of the building, across the street and down a grassy slope to a marshy area. There, squatting on the mud, surrounded by rejected books, was a very large bullfrog. When the chicken dropped her latest offering, the frog looked down, heaved a great sigh, and voiced a response of great dissatisfaction.

"REDDIT! REDDIT!"

In the second such fable, an exuberant young blonde strides into a library. When she reaches the desk, she exclaims, "Hi! I'd like a Big Mac, a large fries and a chocolate shake!"

The librarian, nonplussed, quietly replies, "I'm sorry, miss, but this is a library."

Whereupon the blonde, immediately embarrassed, exclaims, "Oh, I'm sorry! I feel so silly!" Then, leaning forward, she whispers, "Could I have a Big Mac, a large fries and a chocolate shake?"

Tiff and I occasionally tutored some of the guys who helped

us with the gardening and chores. Our very first helper, Doug Bursey Jr., was a leather-clad biker who had dropped out of the educational system towards the end of his final year of high school. When he declared how much he wanted his diploma, I persuaded him to enroll in correspondence French and math courses and tutored him in both. He reached his goal.

A few years later, we took on his younger brother, Ron — both as a worker and a part-time student. He was having so much difficulty improving his marks that I decided to offer him a carrot: if he attained a C average, I would take him on the camping trip his parents never had time for. Given my own work schedule, it was with mixed feelings that I congratulated him for achieving his goal. Shortly thereafter, we packed up the collapsible kayak and headed towards Ottawa. About halfway there, we reached our destination: Bon Echo Provincial Park. Its lake is famous for the native pictographs still visible just above the waterline along some of the cliffs that tower above.

Now, there are two extremes that are not easy for a prairie boy to face — heights and depths, especially if the depths are filled with water. My feelings were not at all mixed when Ron begged we climb one of the cliffs — all the way to the top so we could then look back down at the deep water, so far below. What I felt was pure terror.

But what was I to do?

We found a narrow ledge just above the water and, from it, a chimney (a vertical crevice in the rock) that led all the way to the top.

We got out of the kayak, tethered it to a rock and started up. The chimney was wide enough to accommodate us, one at a time, and uneven enough to provide handholds. Ron led. I began to think that this was not as bad as I had feared.

Then, we reached the top and stood on the very edge.

It was awful, but it wasn't as bad as our return to the bottom. Has anyone ever told you how much more difficult it is to climb down a rock face than it is to clamber up?

Hiring teenage helpers certainly offered mutual benefit, but from the viewpoint of the bosses it wasn't cheap. We had to buy a second fridge and install it in the garage for the cases of soft drinks we kept for them. We also bought Kraft Dinner by the case, as each lad used a whole package at lunch.

When they came to work on Saturdays, I would give them breakfast, usually bacon and eggs, cooked on the griddle of our new restaurant-style gas range. One of the guys always exclaimed how "awesome" the eggs were. (One day I met his mother downtown and all she said to me was: "Okay, Bill. What's your recipe for 'awesome eggs'?")

That we were considered the local sophisticates first came to our knowledge through a call from the owner of Cannington's supermarket. "Can you get right in here? I've got a problem!"

I hurried in, to be taken to a surprising display of avocados, which I had never seen in Cannington before. "Here," the owner said. "Everyone's asking me and I simply don't know. How the hell do you cook these things?"

He was amazed to learn that they were eaten raw.

That same store was the scene of one of my most embarrassing word adventures. I was preparing for the arrival of houseguests — cleaning bed and bathroom linen, prepping for meals, setting the table — when I discovered we were out of the large dinner-size paper napkins we liked to use. So I took a quick break and dashed into the village to get some. To my dismay, I discovered that our store had just gone No Name. Many products were suddenly available only in large yellow and white boxes with black lettering — most of it, for some reason, in French. I scoured the shelves and finally found what I was looking for. I decided this would be a good time to really stock up; I staggered up to the cashier with as many boxes as I could carry and slapped them down on the counter. The cashier just looked at me. I hurried to explain: "I know — it's a lot. But we've got guests. And we're always running out of them. Why, Tiff and I alone can go through one of these in less than a month!" The cashier leaned forward and whispered to me that I was not likely to find dinner-size table napkins in a box labelled "maxi serviettes."

Several Cannington residents provided Tiff with seedbeds for his writing, especially his short stories. One became the heroine of "Funny in Sad Shoes"; another appeared in both the title and the story of "What Mrs. Felton Knew."

Another local life that perhaps should have been fictionalized was that of a retired schoolteacher living in a retired school-house, just down the road. His name was Mr. Irwin.

He was tall and massive, and always wore black. He had a slab-like face that bore a pair of tiny glasses, and was never seen without a large, black leather satchel whose contents would remain a perpetual mystery. He also carried an unsettling aroma about him — vaguely reminiscent of how a butcher might smell.

The first time we met him was when he walked along the road to tell us he'd heard that we sometimes drove to Toronto; he wanted to ask us if we would let him know next time we

were going and if we would drive him as far as Blackwater, a
village about six miles to the south. He had a sister living there.

These drives became a regular feature of our lives. We never
heard how he got back to Cannington. On the rare occasion he
would come all the way into Toronto with us — and all the way
home again. What he did in the city, he never said. He would
always have his black bag with him, and he always rewarded us
— with a chocolate bar we could share.

His voice was high and nasal. Whenever he left us, his slow
departure could be heard for what seemed minutes — a dimin-
ishing series of "Thaaanks ... thanks ... thhhaaaankkks ..."
as he ambled away, usually followed by a platoon of our cats —
possibly attracted by that strange smell.

One day, his niece moved from her Blackwater home and
took up residence with him in the schoolhouse, along with her
husband and young daughter. The two parents seemed to hover
on the edge of mental deficiency, and the little girl was ashen,
sullen, and never dressed warmly enough for cold weather. We
actually alerted Children's Aid about her; they went to investigate. Their report to us was that, although conditions in the
family were not good, as long as the family remained together
there was nothing that could be done.

Eventually, the wife abandoned them and ran off with
another man. Somehow, Mr. Irwin heard that they'd gone up
the Alaska Highway and disappeared. The next thing we heard,
Mr. Irwin had boarded a bus and gone after them.

Months later, he and his niece reappeared. There was never
any word of where she had been, how he had found her, or
who she had been with. Finally, the couple and their daughter
moved back in with Mr. Irwin's sister in Blackwater.

In all the time during which we knew him, Mr. Irwin had two fixations. One was his horror of "total fire" — although he never explained just what he meant by that. The other was his fear that he might be buried in some low spot in a graveyard, where water would seep in, and "the damp" would be his eternal companion. Fire and water.

One severe winter day, two young neighbours discovered Mr. Irwin's body beside his outdoor well. He had had a heart attack while pumping water and was, we were told, frozen stiff. Inside the schoolhouse, his wood-burning stove had scorched the contents of his cooking pots so badly they had to be thrown away.

Mr. Irwin died during the same blizzard through which an ambulance managed to drive me out of Cannington and to the Lindsay Hospital, for surgery to remove a kidney stone.

There was one more Canningtonian who had entered our life: the village's favourite spinster, Islay Lambert. She was a former schoolteacher. In addition to writing a lovely history of the village — *Call Them Blessed* — she also wrote a regular column for *The Cannington Gleaner*.

We became friends with Islay and set up a regular Saturday lunch date with her at her place or ours. We loved going to hers because she still made our favourites from childhood: tuna casserole (with Campbell's mushroom soup and crushed potato crisps) and five-bean salad.

One year, when the village was snowbound and our electricity failed, we had one of our lads get on his snowmobile and take Islay a thermos of hot soup, because we still had the old wood stove as back-up. He had to go twice; the first time, her old hands couldn't unscrew the thermos top.

Our most memorable image of Islay came about when Tiff rode his Honda mini-motorbike into the village (the locals called him "Hell's Elf") to bring Islay to the farm for lunch. Her nosy neighbours had begun to gossip about her shenanigans with those "younger men." Well, curtains really twitched at the sight of Islay, in a crash helmet, climbing on behind Tiff and disappearing in a cloud of dust!

Among our many friends in the Cannington area, there was one who became essential to most of our years there. His name was Len Collins Jr. In the late seventies, as each of us became even busier with our writing, we began to suspect that we needed a change. The system of hiring a series of teenagers as summer help was taking too much supervision. Suddenly, one day a solution to this problem appeared at our door: a young neighbour who was a friend and a contemporary of several of our former helpers — Len.

He was twenty-two, an expert carpenter with a knack for operating and repairing machinery, someone with boundless energy and enthusiasm, and, as we very quickly discovered, exactly what we needed.

We took him on full time and turned over half of our large drive shed to him to use as his carpentry workshop. Over the years, we added annually one more woodworking device to help him produce whatever we needed. This included one of Tiff's favourite pieces of furniture: a huge and superbly crafted partners' desk, at which we sat together whenever we were working on the same project.

Soon, Len married Anne Brandon, a member of one of the two founding families of Cannington. Within a few years, Len, Anne and their three children took over the farm across the road, having purchased it at what we called "a family price."

And indeed, even now, the Collins clan remains a central part of what I call my family.

Another community member who played a key role in our lives was the veterinarian. There were several over the years. They tended to the many ills which the cats, dogs and horses developed. (Twice we rescued old work horses and gave them a retirement home.)

It was, in fact, only a few days after we arrived in Cannington that Tiff made his first call to a vet. We had arrived with one sick cat. During the call, the vet asked questions about the patient, ending with "And where is the animal now?" There was at first only a puzzled silence when Tiff explained, "Right here. On my lap."

Up until that moment, the vet — an expert in agricultural stock — had thought that Tiff had said the call was about a "sick calf."

Inevitably, I had an adventure with a word whose colloquial meaning was known, it seemed, to everyone but me.

We had neighbours who lived beside the little river that crossed our road about half a mile from the farm. When it came time for their daughter to marry, I was asked to deliver the toast to the bride. She was marrying a chap who was both a friend and one of my best technicians at CBC Radio. In my usual inno- cence, I got up and started in on what I hoped would be a gracefully amusing little speech, based entirely on the name of that little river. As I spoke, however, I saw Tiff staring at me with horror and embarrassment, while the bride's father choked on his eighth beer. I had no idea what might be wrong and soldiered on, weaving into my narrative such words as "tail" and "slap" and God knows what else. It wasn't until afterwards, when we got home, that Tiff was capable of explaining to me how my innocent childhood had once again let me down.

The river's name was Beaver.

I finally understood a little routine our teenagers would go through, based on the TV series, *Leave It to Beaver* — the story of a family one of whose sons was so nicknamed. The routine:

"Where's Wally?" (Mr. Cleaver, the kid's father.)

"I dunno. Probably out looking for Beaver!" (Much puzzling laughter.)

In the meantime, Tiff and I continued to write with differing degrees of success. I was discovered by the *Nature of Things* team, whose offices were then located in the CBC Radio Building on Jarvis Street. "What? A writer with two degrees in Biology? Right down the hall?" I was hauled into a film-editing room and asked to fashion a script for a show on bird migration — the first of the over one hundred scripts I would ultimately provide for the series.

The Learning Stage had merged with *University of the Air* to form a new educational series that was first called *The Best Ideas You'll Hear Tonight* — soon and mercifully reduced to *Ideas*, the hugely successful radio series that is still running. That was when I did a series called *The Methods of Madness* in which I interviewed artists, looking for elements of science and/or scientific ways of thinking in their various disciplines: the visual arts, dance, music, theatre. By then, both radio and television were keeping me busy, which meant a hundred-and-fifty-mile commute, three or four times a week.

In the meantime, Tiff had published the novel he had written in the garden of our Richmond Hill home. It had eventually reached a New York editor named Grace Bechtold, who worked for the paperback publisher Bantam Books. She'd liked it, but couldn't publish the paperback until there was a hardcover edition, which took another two years to accomplish. The book finally appeared in 1967.

Then, in 1968, armed with the manuscript of Tiff's second novel, *The Butterfly Plague,* we went down to New York to meet with Grace and with one of Tiff's agents at William Morris. A call from the agent's office announced that he was unable to see us that day, but we were able to take Grace out to dinner and the theatre that evening.

We went to a lovely show at the Lincoln Centre, *Jacques Brel is Alive and Well and Living in Paris.* One song was particularly moving, "Sons." It told of all the sons who suffered early deaths: in war, in accidents, in crime. The young lady who sang it was in floods of tears, and so were we.

The reason the agent didn't feel up to meeting us and why all of New York City was in a state of shock was that Robert Kennedy had been shot in Los Angeles.

The city's grief bordered on the insane. The next morning, seeking respite and calm, Tiff and I retreated to the Bronx Zoo; perhaps the animals there would give us some kind of perspective on the ghastliness. The image I retain of that visit is of a female gorilla, visible behind a glass barrier, sitting on a chair. We watched her eyes as she looked out at the milling, screaming mass of children who had been sent to the zoo as a diversion because their schools had been closed.

On one side of the glass was a maelstrom of out-of-control humanity; on the other side, puzzlement, fear and a measure of resignation — with no loss of dignity.

I would revisit the horrors of Robert Kennedy's death just a few years later, not in New York but in Los Angeles, where the assassination had taken place. It was during a tour of American zoos for a television series I was engaged to write. To give me a chance to visit Los Angeles's Marineland — and to take a break from my travels — I was installed in a famous hotel for three or four nights. It was the Ambassador, in whose kitchens Kennedy had been shot.

My entire stay had a nightmare quality. The Supremes were playing there at the time, and their voices seemed to form a soundtrack I couldn't escape. I went for a walk one evening, wanting to take a look at the La Brea Tar Pits. I soon discovered that nobody in Los Angeles walks. Everyone drives. Anyone walking is viewed with suspicion. I was stopped three times by the police, who demanded identification and my reasons for being on foot. Without reaching my destination, I reluctantly returned to the hotel.

I was reluctant to return to my room for more than one reason. The air-conditioner was leaking, and a gruesome jungle of multicoloured fungi was slowly creeping across the carpet. I notified the desk of this, but nothing was done about it. To me, that insidious rottenness became a symbol of what was happening in American society. I was very happy when I checked out; the horror was just about to reach my bed.

By that time in my life, I was too occupied with film and television documentaries to spend much time with radio. Looking back, I have to admit that it seems remarkable how many scripts I was working on at any given time. So much time and effort was spent travelling back and forth between Stone Orchard and Toronto — to say nothing of all the hours spent running our company, Pebble Productions; handling almost all of Tiff's correspondence; and all of the typing and initial editing of the many drafts he wrote of his fiction.

What made all this possible was the very nature of making a documentary, which took place in stages — some of them quite widely separated in time — providing me with breaks in the heavy workload.

The first stage of creating a documentary was research, which meant a fair amount of reading, often supplemented by long conversations with the producer/director and whatever expert advisor had been engaged. The next stage was then to produce an outline of the show — a detailed indication of what needed to be filmed and the order in which the various aspects of the subject might be presented.

There would then be quite a long hiatus in which the necessary shooting was accomplished, which gave me plenty of time to spend on other projects at various stages of development.

Once the shooting was completed there was a screening of the film, and then the editing began. Often it was the producer who worked with the film editor, choosing and arranging segments, but I soon reached a point at which I could handle that job effectively. This meant I had sporadic sessions with the editor, viewing and helping to refine the cut as we worked to achieve a film of exact telecast length. In between sessions I could either work on other shows, or get ahead on the sound editing. I worked with typed transcripts of segments of the film in which words had been recorded — interviews and any part of the action during which people spoke. I cut and pasted the transcript segments that seemed useful, arranging them in an order that seemed to make sense. Then, the editor and I worked these recorded segments into the footage, using either live shots (of the person speaking) or combining appropriate shots of action with a voice-over of the audio.

Once sound and picture were completely assembled, I then worked with the editor to draw up a shot list, carefully noting the duration of each shot to the half-second, along with an exact transcript of each voiced segment.

While I got to work shaping the narration script, the editor tackled the task of building up the soundtrack, with natural sounds and/or music.

I refined the script over many readings with a version of the film, which would include as much of the soundtrack as possible. The final draft was achieved with input from producer, expert advisor and editor.

Finally, I attended the addition of the narration, which was recorded during a stop-and-start screening that included all of the picture and most of the sound. Frequently my own voice was used for the narration.

In any event, it was the stop-and-start aspect of my involvement in the whole process that allowed me to take on so many overlapping projects. Fortunately, I had learned in the theatre — as stage manager — the techniques of multitasking. With careful management of time, it also gave me the opportunity to have periods of travel — which, ultimately, meant either taking holidays with Tiff or accompanying him on his promotional tours.

We spent the entire summer of 1969 roaming the Northwest Territories. We then owned a Citroen, with seats that could be folded down into sleeping platforms if we were making an overnight stop. For longer stays, we had a lovely two-room tent, with a screened-in sleeping area and a rubberized floor. Our other equipment included sleeping bags and a Coleman kerosene stove with pots, pans, dishes and utensils. Our crowning glory was a collapsible kayak — a German creation called a Folbote — that could be broken down and packed away in three handy cases. From there it could be quickly built up into a wooden framework with a rubberized skin and metal gadgets that allowed it to be snapped together. It even had inflatable gunwales for stability.

It was a fabulous trip: gorgeous lakes and rivers, and magnificent bison in Wood Buffalo National Park. We called one "Caesar," because the first time we saw him he was emerging from a dense growth of trees, a crown of leaves caught on his horns, decorating his brow. The north that summer was somehow free of mosquitoes and blackflies; the only bear we saw was on our way home, just thirty miles north of Cannington!

That summer was the only time I ever grew a beard. It turned out to be a bit of a mistake. On the way back east, Tiff and I stopped off to see my parents in Regina. Usually, such visits entailed lovely meals eaten at favourite restaurants and lots of old friends joining us at the house. This time, there was no socializing. I didn't understand what the problem was until the day, downtown, we saw my mother coming along the street. When she saw us, she quickly crossed over to the other side and continued on her way, head down. I should have known. To my mother, beards meant hippies.

I once sent my parents a dishwasher as a special Christmas present. On my next visit to Regina, I noticed that it looked awfully pristine. So I asked my mother how she liked using it. She was evasive, so I asked her if she had actually used it. She nervously insisted that she did. Then, knowing her well, I asked her how she used it.

The answer finally came: "I keep my purse in it so the hippies don't get it."

It was around this time that my addiction for wordplay took on another dimension. I fell in love with crossword puzzles, especially cryptic crosswords, with complicated clues including puns and anagrams.

Now in my eighties, every morning begins with the daily paper's cryptic. Saturday's gem, designed by someone named Fraser Simpson, is a particular treat.

If friends comment on my apparent ability to solve these, my explanation is simple: "I have learned to speak Puzzlese."

By this I mean simply that I now recognize certain key words in the clue — words that can set me on the right track towards solution.

For example: "back," "up" or "from the right" (or "from the east") prompt me to look at a backward arrangement of some or all of the letters in a possible answer. In a similar way, "wrapped," "covered" or "dressed" make me consider the possibility that the answer consists of one word inserted into the letters of another.

Over the years, I've made a fascinating discovery. Whenever I'm stumped, I "send the problem to committee." By this I mean I set the puzzle aside for a few minutes, and try to engage my concentration in some other activity — reading, watching television, etc. Then, when I return to the puzzle, the answer almost invariably becomes obvious.

Does the subconscious take over when conscious effort fails? It certainly seems so with me. (I invite psychologists to investigate this possibility, if they have not yet done so.)

I have come to suspect that my own subconscious is not only talented, it's mischievous. Can it be that while I'm speaking my subconscious activities manage to stay just far enough ahead of my conscious efforts to be able to foresee the comic possibilities of a slip of the tongue? Could this explain my susceptibility to spoonerisms and other unfortunate utterances?

IN THE EARLY 1970S, WE FOUND a stonemason willing to take on the massive project of building a high stone wall across the front of our lot — dipping lower, right in front of the house, to maintain our view of the fields across the road and ending with pillars that flanked the driveway entrance. We obtained the stones in a deal with neighbours to dismantle two old barn foundations, and we supplemented these with stones drawn from the piles of rocks harvested from our own fields.

The project took three years to complete. The wall was almost built when Tiff had an idea. The wall should contain a time capsule, something that would contain a few samples of our twentieth-century Canadian culture. As the mason worked to lay in the last few stones of the day, Tiff collected his materials. The capsule would be a Coca-Cola bottle containing a few coins (what better symbols of our culture) along with a dated note of explanation. As the mason called out for Tiff to hurry before his mud became too hard, Tiff discovered to his horror that the neck of the bottle was too narrow to receive the coins. In desperation, he found an empty mayonnaise jar, tossed in the coins and the note, screwed on the lid and rushed the whole thing out to the mason, just in time.

It wasn't until the next day that Tiff remembered something

crucial. He hadn't changed the note. It still explained why a Coke bottle was one of our symbols.

I like to imagine a future archaeologist making the astounding discovery of this little aberrant pocket of twentieth-century Canada: the wide-mouthed Coke culture of Cannington.

IN 1971, WE BEGAN WORK ON a wonderfully successful series, *The National Dream*, a docudrama based on Pierre Berton's two histories of the Canadian Pacific Railway. I would handle the documentary aspects and assist the producer in the film-editing, while Tiff would write the dramatic sequences. Early production meetings were memorable for the somewhat bizarre suggestions coming from Pierre, the books' author, and from the series's executive producer, Lister Sinclair.

Pierre was someone we greatly respected as a journalist and popular historian. He was also a commanding six-foot-five, and forceful in his arguments. One day, as we discussed the opening episode — about the early railway surveyors — Pierre revealed an idea he had had. "They all travelled across the vast and forested Laurentian Shield. Now, at that time, those trees would be filled with great hordes of passenger pigeons. Several North American museums and universities still have many mounted specimens in their collections. What I suggest is that we rent as many as we can, take them to whatever location we're going to use and tie them to the branches."

Tiff and I greeted that one with a dignified silence, hoping that our lack of argument might be taken temporarily as agreement. We each had visions of all those dead birds swaying in the wind — some, perhaps, badly fastened in place, hanging upside down. To our relief, the idea simply got lost.

Then, there was Lister — another giant in our world of arts and letters. He was a true polymath; he seemed to know a fair amount about absolutely everything. I had worked with him for years at *The Nature of Things*, and it was he who taught me the didactic principle of good scriptwriting: "Tell them what you're going to do, then tell them that you're doing it and, finally, tell them that you've done it." That may sound dreadfully forced and artificial; but, subtly handled and used only at appropriate moments (such as a transition to a new subject), it proved to be effective.

Lister's Achilles' heel was his love of travel — especially when someone else was footing the bill. I remember one television series he produced and hosted; it featured some of the giants of the music world and was called *Long-Haired Heroes*. No, not the Beatles and their like, but the great classical composers of Europe during the Romantic Era. In content and insight, the series was brilliant; in visual impact, it was dismal. The entire thing was shot from the windows of Lister's rented car as he drove through appropriate countrysides, right past significant buildings. This was the man who would guide the expenditure of our budget.

It was not surprising that it was Lister who had suggestions when planning one of the later episodes. "You remember when there was a financial crisis in 1881. John A. cabled to his right-hand man, Charles Tupper, who was at meetings over in London, 'Pacific in trouble.' And the Prime Minister was so heartened by Tupper's cabled reply: 'Sailing Thursday.' What I propose is that I pick up a film crew in London and take them on the boat train down to Southampton, from which Tupper sailed. We can film out the windows what Tupper saw as headed home!"

This time, I couldn't refrain from argument. "But, Lister," I said, "That was almost a century ago. How can you film 1881 in 1973?"

Lister looked at me, pityingly. "Bill," he said, "of course, I'll film it at night."

I think he was joking.

Since many of those first CPR executives were Scottish immigrants to Canada, Lister also planned to go to Scotland to film Craigellachie, the great rock that was the rallying point for the clan to which some of them had belonged. He would also, he said, get shots that would represent the boyhood of the first CPR president, George Stephen, who loved to stand in the streams of his native Banffshire and cast for salmon.

In the long run, Lister did give up on the boat train footage, but went ahead with Craigellachie and the boy fishing. There were, however, problems with the film he brought back. The great historic rock was absolutely covered with graffiti: JOCK LOVES MARY. UP YOURS. And the only fly fisherman available for the shoot of young Stephen was almost eighty years old.

Then, well before the bulk of the production process, Lister left the project to move to Ottawa, because he had been appointed Vice President of the CBC. It was a good move, I think — for all concerned.

The National Dream was highly successful, earning each of us an ACTRA Award. Following it, Tiff began work on his first full-length play, *Can You See Me Yet?*, and I continued to work in television, occasionally using Stone Orchard as the site for some of the filming.

When I was writing for the teenage series *Drop In*, I brought to the farm one of the series' hosts, Nina Keogh, and a cameraman to take some shots for use in an episode on cows. As an ex-entomologist, I knew that ants "herded" and "milked" aphids. These little "insect cows" clustered on plant stems, sucking up sweet sap. In order to acquire sufficient protein, however, they had to take in a lot of sap, which would provide them with far too much sugar. And so they excreted excess sugar in the form of sticky droplets. Ants can stimulate this process by stroking the aphids with their antennae — in other words, by "milking" them. This we successfully shot.

Then we all went over to the barn next door — a dairy farm owned by a couple who had grown up in Germany. Their son was a teenager, and a gorgeous one. A tall, tanned young man with golden hair and startlingly blue eyes. When I was introduced to him, I thought to myself: "Of course." His name was Siegfried.

Nina interviewed him in the barn, both of them seated in front of the stalls, with a cow standing in the one behind them, facing away. As they chatted, the cameraman and I watched — first in fascination and then with some horror — as something began to appear beneath the cow's lifted tail.

She was giving birth to her calf.

We stopped the shoot and rescued Nina just as the calf's head was approaching her shoulder. Nina was remarkably calm about the whole thing; we simply set up outside with a few other members of the herd and got on with the interview.

(I was especially pleased with that shoot for another reason. The teenage son of other neighbours came to the farm to ask if he might watch some of the shooting, which he did. He was fascinated by it. A few years later, he entered Fanshawe College in London, Ontario, from which he graduated as a television technician.)

Following up on the public's enthusiasm for the railway series, it was decided that Tiff and I would adapt another Berton classic, *The Klondike*, into a longer, fully dramatized series. Each of us wrote six episodes. In early 1974, with the railway series about to be telecast, we travelled by train to Prince Rupert to rendezvous with a CBC team. We boarded a large ferry and sailed through the Inside Passage, which eventually landed us in Skagway, Alaska.

It was a magical trip. Soon, we were passing huge coastal glaciers, at the feet of which the waters teemed with sea life — clouds of tiny crustaceans, fish, orcas and seals. All were attracted to waters made fertile by the action of fresh water meeting salt water, churning up potential nutrients from the sea bottom on which the smaller species fed. The vast numbers of these attracted an astonishing chain of marine life.

On the first night, we were far enough north for the air to retain a silvery leftover from the day. The ship began to thread its way between two islands. The passage was so narrow that soundings were taken in the old way, with someone lowering a weighted cable and calling out the depths — as they once did along the Mississippi, within earshot of Samuel Clemens. "Mark ten." "Mark twelve."

At that moment, someone on the top deck started playing a trumpet — a mournful, magical rendition of "Yesterday." The sound drifted out into the air, a perfect accompaniment to the sounding calls.

Two of our fellow passengers were a young couple heading to Alaska, where they hoped to homestead. They were travelling in a second-hand circus van that housed a horse, a calf, two pigs, some chickens and a hive of bees. When our ship stopped for an hour or so, just offshore of one of the coastal communities, a small boat was lowered and sent in, carrying supplies and mail. The couple carried their hive up onto the lower deck and let it sit there while the bees flew towards the land. "They need to feed and collect food," the couple explained. They assured us that, indeed, the insects could find their way back to the ship before it moved on.

This gave Tiff one of the key final moments in his novel about Noah and the Ark — *Not Wanted on the Voyage* — when the bees are brought out of the hold and onto the deck.

We eventually reached Skagway, from where we would head inland towards the Chilkoot Pass. It had been decided that the first leg of our journey would be accomplished on horseback, which we both found daunting since neither of us had been in the saddle for over twenty years. The timing of the journey was also a bit dicey; it was based on a proposed production schedule rather than on the suitability of travel conditions. It was April; this, as our group quickly learned, created several problems. The spring melt had turned rivers into raging torrents and weakened the deep snow cover we would have to traverse. That was why we were provided with three guides — a snow expert, a rock expert and a river expert. The travel conditions, however, meant that many adventure tourists had also chosen to start out on horseback; there were no pack animals available for the CBC survey and no mounts for the wrangler's wife and young son, who would eventually guide the available animals home when the party needed to proceed on foot.

We were a pretty nervous group when we and all our travel gear were driven out to a beach near Skagway. Troubles were forgotten for a moment, though, when we caught sight of a spawning run of small fish. The whole bay was alive with bald eagles feasting on the abundance. I stopped counting them when I reached eighty. And then I saw the horses, bunched together on the seaside bank of a raging river, which poured its waters across the beach and into the sea.

I was distracted for a moment by the announcement that, without the necessary animals, we would have to wear our forty-pound backpacks in the saddle. How the hell would I maintain my balance with my centre of gravity altered?

With terrible difficulty, I soon discovered.

It took three strong men to boost me up into the saddle, and I came very close to toppling to the ground on the other side of Bandit (yes, that was my horse's name). Bandit didn't want to join the party. He seemed uncomfortable with the feel and the noise of the gigantic coffee pot that he and I were supposed to transport — and he certainly didn't like the feel of an inexperienced, unbalanced rider. So, with me on his back, he turned and headed for home. It took a lot of yelling and yanking to get him stopped and turned around.

When we were all up and ready, our outfitter — who would stay with us for the first day's travels — gave us a pep talk. His name was Skip — a pleasant but somewhat unnerving young man who seemed actually to believe that he was the reincarnation of some 1898 gold seeker.

His first words dealt my confidence an almost fatal blow: "Now, it may look dangerous, but it's really not. Just trust your horse. He knows exactly what to do." Oh? Just what was this dangerous *it*? "All you have to do while we're crossing through the water is …" At that point I stopped listening to anything except to my own inner monologue: *Was he, by any chance, suggesting that we plunge into these frothing, surging waters? On a horse? While trying to balance a heavy backpack?*

Yes. He was.

"Just hang on tight, let your horse do all the work, and you'll be fine. And if you're swept away ..." *Swept away?* "Don't worry ..." *Ha!* "Your horse will eventually get you to the other side." *What the hell do you mean, "eventually?"*

I don't remember the nightmare details of just how we managed it, but we all got across. I do remember thinking that there probably wouldn't be anything quite as bad as what we'd just experienced for the rest of the journey.

"Let's get going. After we cross this island, we ..."

I couldn't believe he'd said "island."

But he had. We somehow survived an even longer stretch of murderous rapids. I don't remember much of what followed, but I do know that at some point I had a brilliant idea. One of us should do the gentlemanly thing and offer a mount to the wrangler's wife.

That was how I safely reached solid ground and proceeded along the trail, contentedly on my own two feet.

It wasn't long before an event encouraged Tiff to join me. While we were making our difficult way over the huge rocks that lined a dry riverbed (the river having cut itself another channel) the horses stampeded. They apparently didn't like the rocks any more than we did. In the rush forward, the upper metal framework of Tiff's backpack was caught by an overhanging branch. A former dancer and actor, he knew how to fall. Getting up, dusting himself off, he followed my example by offering his horse to the wrangler's little boy.

The journey was so much easier on foot. We got quite far

ahead of the rest, because we could thread our way through stands of trees too thick to allow the passage of horses and their riders. We soon had reason to think that perhaps we should stop and wait for the others: we came upon fresh bear dung. Very fresh, green and steaming. We shrugged our way out of our packs and sank, nervous but grateful, to the ground.

I immediately yelled and leapt up. I had managed to land on a very large porcupine quill, which was firmly embedded in my left buttock.

Tiff took over. He helped me ease the weapon out of my clothing as we worked my trousers and underwear to the ground, and then he went to work on the quill, slowly getting it out of my flesh.

That was the moment at which the rest of the party caught up to us, and started to shout out a greeting.

"Hi, guys! Oh. Uhm ..."

A quick explanation, the quill held up in demonstration, and we were on our way again to the camp where we would spend the night and leave our horses.

Soon, we were all out of the trees and above the snow line. It was cold, steep and difficult. The backpacks seemed to grow heavier and the snow became treacherous — sometimes a slippery, slushy horror. There were other times, however, when it was deep and solid enough to offer a relatively easy highway to the heights.

In order not to become dehydrated, we were encouraged to eat frequent handfuls of snow. Since the terrain offered little shelter, though, bladder pressures had to be eased in the open, by dropping back a few feet and letting go.

We learned not to eat red snow, because at those heights there was a poisonous algae, related to that which occasionally caused deadly red tides in southern oceans. There were also dangers hiding beneath the snow.

As we were crossing a long stretch of blissfully solid snow in single file, the guide in front of me suddenly plunged down, up to his hips in snow. I started forward to offer a hand in getting him out, but he stopped me, muttering "Thanks," and the assurance that he was trained to do it himself.

It seemed to take quite a long period of very careful manoeuvring, but finally he was out — and off we went again.

Shortly afterward, he dropped back beside me and quietly explained. "Thanks again, Bill. You should know, though, my feet were dangling in space. I hadn't realized that we were on a huge natural snow bridge and that there was a river far below. I was afraid the whole thing might collapse."

All I could do was nod — and keep plodding forward.

We reached our first key destination: the Chilkoot Pass, a steeply sloping stretch of huge rocks rising up a thousand feet and streaked with lines of melting snow. It lay on one of the major routes used in 1898 to reach the Klondike gold. Thousands of gold-seekers had crossed it as many times as it took them to carry all the gear and supplies they needed to survive the next winter.

We crossed it slowly, clambering over the rocks and resting, occasionally, against the nearest run of melting snow. As hard and heavy as the going was, we eventually reached the summit where we sank to the ground. Now, I'm a prairie boy, which means, as you've read before, that I'm as terrified of heights as I am of swimming in deep water. On the way up, I couldn't bring myself to look back down. Everyone else had, so I finally asked one of the guides to lead me to a point from which I would be able to see the base of the slope — and to let me hang onto him while I took a quick look.

Seeing what we had done was even more terrifying than doing it.

After that, the rest of the trek was relatively easy, but long. The trail had so many switchbacks as it wound up and, occasionally, down over the terrain, that by the time we reached our first community, Lake Bennett, we were almost too stiff to move.

We collapsed on the ground beside a small railway station that served the tourist trade; as we sat there, unshaven, sweaty, dirty and dejected with fatigue, a trainload of elegant (and probably wealthy) American tourists arrived. They spotted us. Apparently thinking we represented the most poverty-stricken members of the local population, they kindly began to offer us leftovers from their lunch packets. I watched as one lady offered Tiff a banana. "Here, you poor thing. I hope you enjoy it." He nodded mutely and began to eat. Given my dire allergy, I was hoping that no one would be so kind to me. I didn't even have the energy to explain.

The rest of the trip was much easier. We embarked on an inflatable Kodiak craft to Whitehorse, and then we travelled by truck to Dawson. The town had been restored and it offered great possibilities for filming, although the surrounding terrain had been thoroughly chewed up by modern machines, used to help retrieve the gold the original hand-digging had missed.

During our stay there, two things had a deep impact on us. The first was the old graveyard; the markers showed just how young so many of the goldseekers had been. The second was the huge outcropping that loomed above it — Midnight Dome.

This is where the prospectors gathered on early summer nights when the sun didn't sink below the horizon. One evening, we climbed up and sat there as the light made a silver wonder of the landscape. Tiff carried his personal mascot all the way to the top — his teddy bear, Sebastian. We took a photograph of the little fellow in that magical light. I grinned to myself, remembering that when we had been asked to jettison non-essentials as the going got tough, Tiff had jettisoned his spare shoes but kept his teddy bear.

On our way back to the coast to catch the ferry that would take us back to civilization, we travelled from Whitehorse to Skagway on the famous narrow-gauge railway through the White Pass, which had been one of the main routes to the gold fields before the railway was built. We were meant to stay overnight at the largest encampment of railroad workers; but, when we pulled to a stop there, all we could see were a lot of police and an even larger group of workers — many of them sporting blood-stained bandages and painful-looking bruises. There had been a riot the night before, with many injuries; our train was to take away ringleaders, the worst casualties, and some of the very young university students who had come north to earn money.

We all travelled on to the next encampment — a smaller one, managed by what turned out to be one of the most memorable women we ever met. When we arrived she met us, wearing her work clothes and apron, and showed us where we would all be sleeping. Tiff and I had assumed we would bunk together, as we did in hotels. Not so. Tiff was shown to the room he would share with one of the injured students, while I was ensconced with my own roommate — one of the ringleaders of the rioting. He was heavily bandaged and sullen, and remained in the room while I went to join the others in a meal.

I was greeted by our hostess, whose name turned out to be Trudy. She was originally from Germany. The apron and work clothes had been replaced by an elegant black dress. Her hair was fluffed up; makeup excellently applied; jewellery discreetly chosen. We were then joined by a few of the students, plus some of the younger railway workers — all of us feeling a bit ashamed, by then, of our lack of better clothes. Trudy soon put us at our ease. She served drinks, initiated conversations and served a splendid meal she had concocted. Afterwards we all played cards. Her very presence somehow transformed us all into gentlemen. We learned, quietly, that this was how the place was run — as an island of gentility in a sea of natural and human wilderness. The next day, we saw further evidence of this. Every time a train passed, Trudy took off her apron, fluffed up her hair, dashed on a bit of lipstick and then stood beside the tracks, waving serenely at the passengers.

After losing every game of cribbage to a young card-sharp of a worker, I finally worked up the courage to return to my roommate. He was still sitting, sullen on his bed. I sat on mine, not knowing what to say. Finally, he spoke. "Gotta smoke?" I pulled out my cigarettes and told him I'd be happy to share them. Slowly, we began to talk. Two hours later, we were still exchanging life stories.

Just goes to show you. Never judge a ruffian on appearances alone. I mean: apart from injuries, did I look any better?

Perhaps of more importance, our stop allowed Tiff to visit a place that, in his mind, was a shrine. It was the site at which two hundred horses had been buried — all victims of accident or exhaustion suffered from carrying the gold-seekers' gear over the White Pass. Tiff would never reveal this during his lifetime, but I think he wouldn't mind if it were known now that one of the dedications in *The Wars* – "To the two hundred" — refers to these tragic animals.

We made our way back to Ontario, where we each wrote a sample script for the proposed series. The scripts were received with enthusiasm, but — sadly — the series was never made. Before any production activity could start, Pierre Trudeau's "tight money" policy came into effect; the project was abandoned. We took what solace we could in remembering the wonders we had seen in the north, but we were also very glad to be at home with our own animals.

Maggie, our first dog, had died shortly before we left for the Yukon, leaving her son, Hooker, alone. He was inconsolable; he wouldn't eat, wasn't interested in walks. He just lay there, his head on his paws.

Finally, Tiff said: "We've got to do something. C'mon."

We went to the dog pen and persuaded Hooker to follow us out onto the lawn. We went over to where a stile lay across the cedar rail fence, providing access to Tiff's herb garden. He and I sat on the steps, while Hooker sat down, dejected, at our feet.

"Now what?" I asked.

"This …" And Tiff threw his head back and started to howl.

I just looked at him — and then, I began to howl.

Within seconds, Hooker joined us. The three of us sat there, howling, until somehow, we all seemed to think we had paid Maggie her due. When we were silent, Hooker's tail began to wag. After that, he was just fine.

OUR ANIMALS SEEMED TO HAVE QUITE a cordial relationship with the local wildlife. Except for a privileged few living in the house, most of the cats spent their days outside and their nights sheltering in the partly heated pool pump shed. We called them the outdoor crew, and fed them on the front porch, using long containers fashioned from eavestrough. And there we would often see a mother raccoon, who would bring her kits to play with our crew while she feasted on cat food.

During one particularly hot and dry summer — when we were careful to keep all the water dishes filled — we saw Moth, the daughter of Max and Mouse, lead a strange cat all the way from the back field up to a water bowl on the porch. We first thought it was a cat. It turned out to be a very thirsty groundhog.

LIFE AT STONE ORCHARD WAS ABOUT to change, thanks to a call Tiff received from Ottawa. By then, Jean Roberts and Marigold Charlesworth were at the National Arts Centre — Jean as Director of Theatre and Marigold as Director of English Theatre.

The purpose of their call was to invite Tiff to become the Centre's first playwright-in-residence. It would mean spending the last three months of 1974 at the Centre — observing rehearsals, meeting actors and other writers, and working on a new play of his own. Having written for over five years and many months without being able to come up with a novel that anyone wanted to publish, Tiff was excited by the thought of returning to the theatre. He quickly accepted the invitation. All he needed, then, was time to think about what he might write for the Centre.

He had been publishing short fiction during those dry years, as well as creating radio documentaries and one radio drama titled "Missionaries." That, he decided, is what he would reshape for the stage.

He moved into an Ottawa apartment hotel and got to work. I would drive over to visit him every few weeks — whenever I could release myself from the various television documentaries on my schedule. As we both knew, there would inevitably be some falls from grace that would involve drinking, but we had survived plenty of these episodes together and were confident we could cope with whatever might happen while we were apart. Such an episode is described in one of Tiff's later books — based on excerpts from his journals — *Journeyman: Travels of a Writer*. The episode was an invasion we suffered during one of my visits. Four young hooligans Tiff had met at a bar in Hull forced their way into our apartment and terrorized us for an hour, until Tiff managed to escape and call the police.

It was during rehearsals for John Coulter's epic play, *Riel*, that Tiff came up with an idea of how to transform "Missionaries," which was the story of a failed missionary with a troubled family. Tiff's idea was to set the story in an asylum for the insane, where the woman would, in her mind and behaviour, turn her fellow inmates into the family members she remembered (or — since this was Findley — the family members she might be inventing). To the great joy of us both, his revised script was accepted for production in the 1976 season of the Centre.

Tiff returned to Stone Orchard. To everyone's surprise and initial concern, I left for Ottawa.

It was a perfectly cordial parting, because we both knew our separation would be only temporary. While Tiff continued to wrestle with new fiction, I spent a few months at the Centre, helping Jean Roberts through the difficulties and frustrations of producing theatre in an organization that was part of the civil service. As she put it to me, "The bureaucrats demand to know how many hats we will need for the next season's plays, long before we've chosen which plays we'll produce!" Along with her supervision of complete theatre seasons in both official languages — comprised of both in-house and invited productions — she was also expected to deal fully and tactfully with reactions to the productions from the critics and the public, as well as to develop new playwrights and run outreach programs designed to interest young people in the theatre.

I took the title of Assistant to the Director of Theatre, moved into an Ottawa apartment and got to work.

Inevitably, Tiff had a few wild periods back at Stone Orchard, but nothing lasting too long or causing too much damage of any kind. As for me, I never managed to find any new plays or new playwrights; none of my excursions across the country turned up any productions with both worth and availability for transfer to Ottawa. I did, however, manage to do for Jean what I continued to do for Tiff — take over the correspondence and free the artist to get on with the important work.

I even managed to get on a bit with my own. I had been able to arrange it so that, as long as I was in Ottawa, I would not be expected to work on any Toronto documentaries — but I did get an interesting call from a producer at the National Film Board in Montreal. He was preparing a documentary for CIDA, the Canadian International Development Agency (the former phrase, "foreign aid," was no longer fashionable). What this producer proposed was bizarre enough to interest me. His personal views on development were diametrically opposed to those of

CIDA, and he was looking for a writer who could provide a script that would be perceived by the government as expressing CIDA's views, but to an audience would actually articulate the producer's own ideas.

I thought I'd give it a try; putting words together in such a way so that both sides of an argument would be satisfied appealed to me. I was able to work in my spare time, using the VCR in my apartment. It took a few weeks; when I went to Montreal to try the script out on the producer — with his copy of the film — he was pleased. He then set up a screening and reading for CIDA executives. They were pleased. I went back to Ottawa, also pleased — and considerably amused.

The next morning, I got a call from Montreal. "I've been thinking, Bill; if they like it, it just can't be saying what I want it to say. I've arranged to have all the rough footage copied. We'll start all over again, from scratch."

My reply consisted of just two words. I never saw the chap again. No, not those two words. All I said was: "Good luck." And hung up.

IF YOU WORK IN THE THEATRE, you are bound to meet some pretty interesting characters. One whom I encountered in Ottawa was the wife of one of the Centre's executives — a vivacious, wide-eyed creature with an abiding love of martinis. In one way or another, she was the life of every NAC social occasion.

I have vivid memories of one reception held in honour of a visiting company of players. Helen — as I will call her — was in her usual state of slightly slurred speech and glassy gaze.

"Darling!" she exclaimed as she approached. "Did you hear about Hal?" (As I will call him.) "Well, as you know," (I didn't) "he was in Seattle last week an' he went to this Chinese restau-ran', an' he started to choke! It was awful! An' then this waiter appeared an' did the thing — you know — the whassis man-oeuvre," (Heimlich, I muttered to myself) "an' he put his arms around Hal from behind and gave *huge squeeze!*"

At that moment, illustrating a motion while holding a full martini glass, she managed to toss its contents over her shoulder onto the back of the neck of a chap standing behind her. She turned, at first puzzled, and then contrite. "Oh, darling, I'm so sorry! I ... what? You would? Oh, sweetheart, that would be wonderful." She handed him her empty glass, turned back to me, and started all over again. "Well, you see ... Hal was in Seattle and went to this Chinese ..." and so forth. In the middle of it, her martini glass was returned, full. "Oh, my love. That's marvelous. Thank you so much ..." Back to me. "Oh, yes ... well, Hal was in Seattle and he went ..." I listened to the whole story all over again. This time, when she reached the moment of the manoeuvre, she expertly tossed an entire martini onto the back of one of our female guests. In the ensuing uproar, I managed to creep away.

In the spring of 1976, Tiff's play had its premiere. *Can You See Me Yet?* was directed by Marigold Charlesworth. The stellar cast of eleven included dear friends such as Frances Hyland and Amelia Hall. Audiences, the National Arts Centre, and many civil servants were delighted. The critics were not.

It was almost universally slammed. It has never been given another professional production; although, with eleven chal-lenging roles, it is still frequently revived by amateur theatre.

Tiff, understandably, was shattered by what the critics wrote and broadcast. As was I, but I had to find something to say to him.

Perhaps there was nothing that could immediately lift his spirits, but there might be something to put the whole situation into perspective.

As a special treat for our elderly Cannington friend, Islay Lambert, we had arranged for her to come to the play's opening. We first took her shopping on Bloor Street in Toronto, where she found a gorgeous gown — navy blue with big white butterflies. At the last minute, though, her trip to Ottawa had to be cancelled because of ill health. Now it was time to tell Tiff the truth.

I sat him down with a glass of wine and told him why Islay had not been there on opening night. She had had a heart attack and was dead. Tiff was silent. Tearfully, he said "Yes ..."

And after a few moments, in a stronger voice: "Yes. That matters. This doesn't ... at least, not so much ..."

After that, although the disappointment remained, the despair did not.

Tiff soon returned to the farm, while I stayed on in Ottawa for another year. We visited frequently with each other, either in Ottawa or Cannington.

As Tiff published in his first memoir, *Inside Memory*, it was during one of his visits to Ottawa that he woke up one morning with a glorious idea for a new novel. It was not to be the dark and dreary stuff of the three earlier attempts, he said, but a strong and positive story. What he excitedly described to me was the story of a young Torontonian who goes off to World War I, is horribly maimed by fire, and dies.

That was the birth of *The Wars* — considered by many to be Tiff's finest novel.

Of course, my first reaction that morning was a stunned

silence. By the time I was able to start typing the early drafts, however, I saw just how strong and positive it was. Its writing took Tiff just three months. It was the only one of his books for which I was not able to provide all the typing; the time frame was too limited and the distance between us too great. Most of the manuscript was typed by Tiff's friend at The Writers' Union of Canada, Ellen Powers.

By then Tiff had a new agent, Nancy Colbert, whom he had known during his California days. She got him his first Canadian publisher, Clarke Irwin. The published version of *The Wars* was almost completely identical to his original submission. There had been only two editorial suggestions: a minor change in a paragraph about Robert Ross's father and a short introductory scene that would bring the War into the novel at the outset.

At that time, it seemed that Tiff's fiction was awash with alcoholic mothers; here was one again — Mrs. Ross. When I first read the new introductory part, my heart fell. "She was standing in the middle of the railroad tracks. Her head was bowed ..." Had Tiff — for some bizarre reason — taken Robert's mother all the way to the Front? Then I read the rest of the sentence, and breathed a huge sigh of relief.

"... and her right front hoof was raised, as if she rested."

Hallelujah!

When a feature film was made of *The Wars*, Tiff wrote the script and we visited a couple of the shoots. One took place in a Hamilton mansion which had achieved historic status, and was temporarily to act as the Toronto home of Robert Ross. The film was being directed by Robin Phillips who, as we soon observed, had his own way of achieving the performance moments he wanted.

The scene we watched was set in the Ross dining room, following the accidental death of Robert's damaged sister, Rowena, who had fallen from her wheelchair while she was in the barn visiting her pet rabbits. Robert had left her unattended for a few moments.

The scene was a three-hander, with Brent Carver as Robert and Martha Henry and Bill Hutt as his parents. Just before it began, we saw Robin dash onto the set and whisper something to Martha. Her face froze — and remained that way for the rest of the take. The camera remained trained on Martha throughout the scene. When there was a break, we joined her outside for a cigarette. Tiff asked her what on earth Robin had said to produce such an effect. She paused and then said, cold as ice: "He said, 'You have just given birth … and it's dead.'"

In the next take, the camera was to be on Brent. Again, Robin dashed in for a last-minute comment. To our puzzlement, the comment was again directed at Martha.

Here's the dialogue that was being filmed:

MARTHA: The rabbits must be killed.
BRENT: But, Mother … why?
MARTHA: Because they were hers.
BRENT: (long pause) But … who … who will kill them?
MARTHA: (a loud and violent shout) YOU WILL!

The shout was in obedience to what Robin had whispered to her. Its sudden loudness produced on Brent's face an expression of utter shock. Just what Robin wanted.

The next shoot we attended was in a huge studio, with a

large area filled with mud and replicas of human corpses, crows apparently feeding on them. The battlefield.

What I remember most about the shoot was not the action itself, but the fact that the commissary — all those tables of goodies and various refreshments for the cast and crew — was set up right beside the pile of spare corpses and the cages of extra crows, plus a few cages of shuffling rats — just in case. Nobody else at all seemed to notice or care.

IT WAS MY MOTHER, IN A sense, who ended my stay in Ottawa. By 1977, my parents were living in an apartment in Markham, Ontario — close to my stepbrother, Jim Thomson, and Jim's wife, Fran. That spring, my stepfather died — and although Fran Thomson in particular was exerting every effort to offer support to my mother, I thought it was time to move back to the farm and be more readily available to help. Mother was already showing signs of the senility that would ultimately immobilize her.

While Tiff launched himself into a novel about the rise of fascism during the thirties, *Famous Last Words*, I continued writing for the CBC and occasionally for a few independent producers. Tiff joined me in one CBC project — a somewhat theatrical documentary contrasting attitudes and settings in the published works of two Francophone writers, Gabrielle Roy and Marie-Claire Blais: the heartwarming family stories of Mme. Roy, set in Manitoba, versus the dark and somewhat bizarre stories of Marie-Claire, set in Quebec. For the title, we borrowed a phrase from another writer who had written about them: *The Garden and the Cage*.

The result was moderately successful. We were asked to write another. We came up with what we thought was quite a nice idea: the work of Margaret Laurence — gentle family stories set in a fictionalized version of her Manitoba childhood — contrasted with the far more cerebral tales of Robertson Davies, set in an equally fictionalized version of his hometown in Ontario.

The CBC "Brass" (as they were called by most of us) loved the idea of Davies, but dismissed Laurence as "parochial." They said they "needed an internationally famous writer, here." Somewhat facetiously, I made a suggestion that I thought had no real value at all. "You mean someone like Iris Murdoch?"

"Terrific!" was the response. "Do it!"

I got to spend an afternoon with Iris Murdoch. I was sent to London to interview her in the CBC studios there. When I arrived, I was delighted to find that the cameraman assigned to me was an old friend originally from Germany, Lutz Dille. While we waited for our guest to arrive, we caught each other up on our lives since the last time we'd met — at the Red Barn Theatre, over ten years earlier.

Miss Murdoch was a bit late. While we waited, I thought about all twenty-nine of her novels I had read — including the latest one, *The Sea, The Sea*. I also imagined that she would probably resemble the fiction she had created — elegant, sophisticated, absolutely charming. The last resemblance I imagined was apt. What hurried into the studio was a little lady with straight, iron-grey bangs and a harried look. She needed to get away to visit her ancient mother in a home. She wore two dresses — a light, short-sleeved dress over a heavier long-sleeved one — and had an elastic bandage around one knee. She carried two very full string shopping bags.

We quickly settled into the interview and were well into it

when there was a Germanic shriek from behind the camera. "*Mein Gott*! I forgot the film!"

Iris and I waited until Lutz had loaded the camera. I was thinking: *I've got to put this lady at her ease.* Now, it happened that before I had left for London, Tiff had discovered an article by Dame Rebecca West about current female writers in Britain. Having very much enjoyed the piece, I asked Miss Murdoch if she was familiar with it.

"No," she said. "What did Rebecca have to say about me?"

"I'm afraid I can't quote it exactly, but I can certainly paraphrase it."

She nodded.

"'In a typical Murdoch novel, we are taken to a rather dreary London suburb, to a somewhat dilapidated mansion, on the ground floor of which a middle-aged couple are making love. On the second floor, another middle-aged person, wearing repulsive underclothing, has either just succeeded or just failed in committing suicide, while on the top floor, an adolescent boy, deaf and dumb but, as it will turn out, terribly attractive to homosexuals, is skinning a goat.'"

I laughed — encouragingly and appreciatively.

Miss Murdoch had become increasingly stern. With a forced smile, she announced, firmly, "Still, I'm sure she meant it kindly."

I am happy to report that by the end of the interview, Iris and I were back on cordial terms.

Sadly, I don't have anything very positive to say about the resulting program. It wasn't a good idea to begin with. In spite of a lot of excellent advice from a lot of excellent people, it is a project that Tiff and I rarely mentioned.

What I would like to mention is the style of documentary narration I used. I've outlined the overall process of making a documentary — the various stages, with plenty of time between them for the writer to work on other projects — but there's also something to say about the process of the writing itself.

Any writer faces the repeated challenge of finding that elusive necessity, the right word. Right in meaning and nuance, certainly, but also right in its rhythm. It must fit perfectly into the music of the writing. And, for the documentary writer, it must also fit the various rhythms of the film. Some of these rhythms involve sound, including the sounds produced by the action in any shot, recorded during the shooting. There are also the rhythms of any music that may be chosen to accompany a sequence of shots.

Perhaps even more important are the visual rhythms — the cadence of the actions within a shot, of camera movement, of cuts from shot to shot. All of this is why I used to say that my job was to write the lyrics to visual music. It is also why I was glad to be the one to voice the narration. After spending hours choosing the words while watching the picture, then repeatedly reading the narration aloud while the producer, sponsor and others watched the picture — who better to time utterances and breathing so precisely? Who better to sing these lyrics so appropriately?

There was a lot to be learned about such writing and sometimes the education was accidental. One such lesson involved the actress Patricia Neal, who came to Toronto to narrate a script I had written for an episode of *The Nature of Things* about stroke survivors — of which she was one. Unfortunately, her agent had not informed us that, although Miss Neal's recovery was astounding, there had been one notable change in her speech patterns. The rate at which she spoke had been reduced by about a third. Since my script was tightly keyed to the rate of change from one shot to another, this meant the script had to be reduced to the same degree — by a third. I sat in the recording booth with the actress, cutting words on the wing as we went. This is when I learned that a narration script need not be based only on complete sentences. A series of phrases could, in fact, increase clarity and impact. Further exploration of this idea convinced me that it is often the action of the film that supplies the verbs — and helps to make those verb-less phrases work.

Another of the writer's jobs was to devise a title, something I enjoyed. For a *Nature of Things* on the relationship of bodily fluids to the salt water from which we evolved, I suggested "Blood, Sea and Tears." For a series on the uncertainties of youth employment: "Future Tense." Once, when I was asked to write a script for a short film on the creation of soundtracks for dramatic films, I turned the job down, telling the producer that his documentary didn't need a script. He was appalled. "But how will the audience be able to understand what's going on?" I explained. Most of the film was split screen — half showing the dramatic action and half displaying the sound man creating the final soundtrack: coconut shells on sawdust-filled pads for hoof beats, smashing a cabbage onto a table for a blow to the head, etc. Then I said, "Look. Instead of hiring me to write a script, how would it be if I simply gave you a title and a subtitle, free of charge?" He was puzzled, until I told him what I had in mind: *Track Stars: The Unseen Heroes of Movie Sound.*

The unscripted film won a nice award — and certainly not because of the title alone. It was a good piece of work.

What I found, over the years, was that the three hours or more I spent getting from home to work and back were invaluable in solving the challenges in the choice of words — for scripts or titles. I learned to split my attention between the driving and the pondering just enough.

There was one project in my career about which I usually have little to say. Certainly, I never name names. CBC material was usually edited in house, but if no corporate editor was available we often went to a private company: Film Arts, on Church Street, in the heart of what is now known as The Village — the gay centre of Toronto. It was co-owned and run by a miracle of a man, Don Haig, who, sadly, died just a few years ago.

I was there, working on an episode of the teeny-bopper series *Drop In*, when I received what I first thought was an unacceptable offer. Someone I had never met wanted me to be one of the writers of material for a political campaign, on behalf of a party I would not support. What integrity, eh? Well, integrity gave way to practicality when I discovered how much money was being offered — more than enough to buy a new car.

I'm not going to tell you which campaign it was, which candidates or who had the ultimate approval of the material. Not to protect the innocent or the guilty, but more to avoid the powerful. I will admit, however, that the whole project involved both provincial and federal politics before it was over.

My job turned out to be the editing and scripting (with only sparse voice-over material) of what they called "streeters" — brief interviews with potential voters encountered on the streets of Toronto. It was relatively easy work, but I had to wait until after midnight each day for it to be approved. For

some reason, the person in charge wanted to keep his involvement totally secret.

The first step in approval happened a bit earlier than midnight. It involved a battery of young lawyers, all wearing jeans
and running shoes. They would crowd into the editing room,
say dreadful things about the candidate and his appearance and
never agree on an opinion regarding what they were watching.
Then they'd all go out for a drink.

One night, I was particularly anxious to leave. I had to get
home to pick up some material for my other work the next
day. Around 11:30 p.m. I asked the second-in-command if he
knew when the big boss was intending to arrive. The trouble
is, I used the boss's name. Out loud.

What I got back was: "Shhhhh! Never say his name! Never!
Anywhere!"

"You're kidding."

"No I'm not kidding. Call him 'Uncle'!"

"You're kidding!"

"Call him 'Uncle'!"

Pause.

"Okay. What time is Uncle coming?"

Then, with a sigh of relief and a smile: "He should be here
about half past midnight."

He was.

I finally got home.

I ultimately bought that new car. And that was just for the
first of the three campaigns I worked on. But after the third one
— the national one — I never did it again.

Occasionally, I would encounter astonishing naïvety among
my colleagues in documentary work. The first time was when

I flew to Arizona with the producer of a film about an artist who depicted scenes of native life in that area.

We had to change planes in Chicago; for the first and last time in my entire flying career, the gate at which we landed was right next to the gate from which we would leave. And so I hustled off to the washroom for a couple of minutes. When I got back, my colleague was talking to a new passenger, who accompanied us to Phoenix. When I heard what he was saying to this passenger, I pretended I was with someone else.

"Uh — are you a musician?"

"Oh, yes."

He laughed. "I thought so! Most of you people are."

Oh, Lord. He was talking to Ella Fitzgerald.

She was invited by the pilot to come onto the intercom and scat-sing us down into our landing.

Heavenly woman!

WE FILMED MY INTERVIEW WITH THE artist. On the flight back, the producer turned to me and said: "You know, Bill, there was one moment I really enjoyed."

I was immediately nervous. "Oh, really? Which one?"

"When you asked him what he particularly liked about what he did."

I swallowed.

"I don't think we can use that bit."

"Why on earth not? I was fascinated."

I then had to explain the difference between what the artist meant and what he actually said. The difference between "manual labour" and "a hand job."

But then, who am I to talk? I've been just as guilty of that kind of thing, of being too innocent.

I remember a *Nature of Things* that examined the social structures that had evolved in one species of monkeys. It was a matriarchal system in which males were awarded their social position according to the status achieved by their mothers in physical combat. How could I express this with the greatest economy — and the greatest punch? I had a brilliant idea. In my childhood, I often heard someone brag: "I bet *my* ole man can lick *your* ole man!" In the draft of the script I first read to the producer — a woman — I declared that, among these monkeys, male status was determined on the basis of "my ole lady can lick your ole lady!"

She stopped the film and turned to me. "Bill, you can't say that."

"Whyever not? Isn't it accurate?"

"Ummm … no. Not exactly."

Suddenly, I twigged. I had completely forgotten about the existence of oral sex.

It's so easy to write or say something that fails to convey the intended meaning. I think of it as the potential treachery of words.

I remember watching a television documentary about the massive annual migration of caribou across our north. Its production involved several people I greatly admired — including the actor chosen as narrator. Shortly into my viewing, however, it became apparent that the shooting of the film had suffered a serious setback. It had apparently been impossible to locate the main herd, which would number in the tens of thousands or more. The film was able to follow only a small band of twenty or thirty animals. To make matters worse, this band was traversing fairly benign terrain — no mighty rushing rivers, no precipitous slopes — just flat, rather dull countryside, broken only by the occasional stream. Worst of all was the narration itself. What we heard must have been written well before the shooting, in the expectation of vast numbers and insurmountable difficulties. The narrator — an accomplished radio actor — infused his voice with all the drama and tension that the producers must have hoped for, but never found.

The result was a dreadful, almost farcical quarrel between what we were watching and what we heard. Pictured was a small troupe of caribou ambling into a knee-high, slowly moving stream; less than half a minute later, they strolled out of the water to continue on their way. What we heard, delivered with passion and suspense, in a booming voice, was "AND THEN, WITH LITTLE PAUSE, THE MIGHTY HERD PLUNGES INTO THE ROILING WATERS."

To make matters even worse, I was immediately presented with an utterly ridiculous image. For some reason, instead of "pause" I heard "paws." *With little paws, the mighty herd ...*

WHILE TIFF WAS STRUGGLING WITH FAMOUS *Last Words*, his monumental novel about the rise of fascism in Europe during the thirties, we were asked to be the writers for an impressive CBC project: two ninety-minute documentaries about the Canadian raid on Dieppe in World War II. Tiff felt he couldn't do much of anything until his novel was closer to completion, so we worked out a deal with the producer, Terence Macartney-Filgate. As co-writer I would work closely with the film editor, structuring the story, as I usually did as writer alone, and then

— in collaboration with Tiff — we would provide whatever narrative was needed in the final stages.

The plan was to take sixty veterans of the notorious raid back to Dieppe and film their accounts of where and how they had participated in the event. Tiff and I were a bit concerned about how much they still remembered — and how much they would be willing to tell. We had each known World War I veterans — none of whom had been willing to tell very much about the horrors of trench warfare. We soon discovered, though, that participants in the more recent war were not only eager to talk about it — they remembered practically everything, having kept their memories alive through regular get-togethers with former comrades.

Neither of us had ever been to Dieppe, so it was decided that I would fly over with one group of the veterans. (Tiff, at that time, refused to fly — he had had a bad flight experience years before.) My flight was in an old Royal Canadian Air Force troop carrier, its interior stripped to the minimum, a couple of apples and water the only refreshments on offer. All across the Atlantic, my companions on the flight — true to their nature — exchanged stories about the 1942 raid, which led to a deeply disturbing moment.

You have to understand something of the history of the event as background to what I experienced. The raid should never have happened as it did — and probably shouldn't have happened at all. Dieppe's location and nature made it easy for the Germans to turn it into an impregnable fortress — a wide-open beach, flanked on either side by cliffs, with artillery batteries everywhere on the heights above and along the street that bordered the beach. But due to pressure from Canada, whose soldiers had been idling in Britain for months, and pressure from Britain, anxious to test the possibilities of a massive invasion across the English Channel, a plan of attack was eventually drawn up — a very silly plan, in the opinion of many.

A huge armed flotilla would make a nighttime crossing of the Channel, from which a massive dawn raid would be launched: landing craft carrying infantry and tanks would land on the beach, supported by simultaneous attacks from the air and from offshore artillery. As back-up, an entire regiment of soldiers from Quebec, the FMR (Les Fusiliers Mont-Royal), would also be held offshore, to be sent in at the first sign of successful penetration of the town's defenses.

The vast, open stretch of the beach became an infantry slaughterhouse. The tanks, having practised on sandy beaches in Britain, were immediately immobilized on Dieppe's beach of large stones.

Only a handful of soldiers — and no tanks at all — made it all the way across the beach and into the town. One group of four from a Windsor regiment was among them. Their radio operator sent a signal to the command ship offshore, telling of this small success. In the noisy uproar of the battle, however, the message was misunderstood. Commanders believed that the entire regiment was in the town. The order was immediately given: send in the FMR!

They were destroyed. Their leader, General Menard, received five wounds while wading ashore. He watched as almost half his men were gunned down in waters that slowly turned red with their blood.

On the flight to Europe, I was seated between two of the veterans who had been involved in that moment of the raid; on my right was General Menard and on my left was the Windsor soldier who had sent the misinterpreted message.

It was the most uncomfortable flight I've ever had. Thankfully, by the time we landed, the old bitternesses had been resolved. We were able to get to work.

Working on *Dieppe: 1942* remains one of my best memories of documentary writing. After more than a year's editing of the 30,000 feet of footage, the final documentary series was hailed as one of the CBC's finest productions.

Meanwhile, writing *Famous Last Words* was continuing to frustrate Tiff, so he set it aside for a while to undertake a piece of theatre. He had had a call from his old friend, William Hutt, who had played Sir John A. Macdonald in *The National Dream.* Hutt wanted Tiff to write a play about our first prime minister to be produced at the Grand Theatre in London, Ontario, where he was artistic director. Tiff would give it the title *John A., Himself.*

The script was completed fairly quickly. The first act was in the style of Victorian Music Hall, in which John A. appeared as a famous actor being feted on the eve of his retirement. Parliament was seen as a troupe of acrobats constantly failing to form a human pyramid. The press was represented by a ventriloquist with a John A. doll, which would speak whatever its manipulator wished to have said. There were patter songs in the style of Gilbert and Sullivan. The climax of the act involved John A. and Louis Riel as acrobats fighting it out, balanced on the top edge of a giant map of Canada.

The second act was written as Victorian melodrama; it told of John A.'s private life — the childhood murder of his young brother, the early death of his son, the birth of a daughter inflicted with lifelong disability and the effect of his drinking on both his private and public life.

It was a stunning piece, wonderfully produced. Sadly, it attracted little attention. Like his first play, *Can You See Me Yet?*, it has not had another professional production.

Books and scripts continued to be completed at Stone Orchard, but it wasn't all work at the farm. There were many visitors — and a great deal of entertaining.

The greatest number of guests we ever sat in our dining room was ten, which, with us, made twelve. This was for one of our celebrations of July First, Dominion Day. And although we started out as twelve, an unexpected guest arrived at the last minute, which created a serious problem for Tiff and his superstitions. "We can't be thirteen at table!" he moaned.

I thought for a moment and said, "Okay, you set another place. There's room at the far end of the third table. I'll be right back." I hurried into the front hall and fetched our fourteenth guest.

It was the John A. puppet from the ventriloquist's act in Tiff's play. We had purchased it after the final performance and installed it on an old church pew in the front hall — to welcome visitors and, as it turned out, to confuse my mother on her visits during her mental decline. (She would always pause, uncertain, and then utter a cautious: "How do you do ...")

We celebrated that particular Canada Day with a meal watched over by our first prime minister.

THE FARM HAD MANY VISITORS WITH recognizable names. For a few years, a regular Christmas visitor was Al Boliska, once a well-known Toronto disc jockey. He was brought by one of my oldest friends from my Saskatoon days, Beverley Roberts, who became Tiff's researcher. They always brought another visitor: Sarah.

Sarah's appearance elicited much comment from Tiff, me and other visitors. She was big, blonde and billowy. Sarah appeared only at mealtimes, spending most of her time upstairs. Al was particularly fond of her.

Quite simply, Sarah was the name the couple had given to Beverley's outrageously oversized wig.

After Al's death, we never saw Sarah again.

It wasn't until the 1980s that two innovations reached Stone Orchard. The first was a good water supply, the result of our ability, finally, to afford to have a deep well drilled. With all that water, we could have the other innovation — a dishwasher, which I always referred to as one of our household gods.

I cherish the memory of discovering that our dishwasher had powers to solve one of the few problems we had with our neighbours at Stone Orchard — unwelcome evangelism. The story involves a clever little mouse who was able to get into the dishwasher and feast on whatever might be found on the dishes before the washing began. How it got in, I don't know — since water couldn't get out. One morning, I was in a bad mood. I was having trouble with a script, the phone kept ringing, and it was almost time to leave everything to make lunch.

Then I heard rather timid knocking at the front door. My desk faced a window looking out onto the porch. I could see what we most dreaded: pale faces and pamphlets. The Jehovah's Witnesses had come again — despite our repeated pleas they leave us to our own beliefs, whatever they might be.

As I headed to the door to explain our stance yet one more time, I passed the dishwasher, which I had loaded with dishes and soap but not yet turned on. I crankily flipped the switch and carried on to the porch door. Just as I opened it, I remembered. "Oh, Christ! I forgot the mouse!"

Leaving the visitors to stare and wonder, I dashed back and swung open the washer door. And there was the mouse — soaked, but still in good health. I quickly grabbed a tea towel and managed to pick the animal up. "I'll be right with you," I called. "I'm just drying the mouse!"

I released the creature onto the floor and headed back out into the hall. I looked. Nobody was there.

I guess they had decided I was beyond redemption.

(I confess I did re-enact this a couple of times, but without the mouse, for other representatives of the same group. I achieved the same positive result.)

The other household god was the computer. Finally, I was released from retyping complete drafts of novels. And the computer could do other tricks, too.

During the writing of *Not Wanted on the Voyage*, Tiff wanted to change the name of a leading character. In early drafts, Noah's wife was referred to simply as "Mrs. Noyes," an acknowledgement that the bible failed to supply names for any of the female characters in the story of the Flood. Tiff tried calling her "Marguerite;" but, in the end, he didn't find that suitable. He wanted to return to "Mrs. Noyes."

"Don't worry," I told him. "Now that's simple. The computer has a feature called 'Find and Replace.' I'll ask it to search for all mentions of 'Marguerite' and replace each one with 'Mrs. Noyes'!"

Which I did, forgetting a sentence that read: "Noah's wife's name was Marguerite Noyes." And so the novel almost went to the publisher with this somewhat confusing sentence: "Noah's wife's name was Mrs. Noyes Noyes."

ALL THROUGH THESE DECADES, MOST SUMMERS saw us at the same Maine seaside resort that had received the Findleys since before World War I. It was called Atlantic House, and would be the setting of Tiff's 1986 novel, *The Telling of Lies*, his only mystery, which featured the amateur detective, Vanessa Van Horne. She was based on an unforgettable Atlantic House friend from New York, Dorothy Warren. There were others there who were no less memorable.

FOR YEARS, I HAVE WORN A ballpoint pen on a cord around my neck. I was constantly in need of a pen as I rushed from editing room to editing room, but seldom wore clothing with a breast pocket in which one could be carried. Hence the cord. It also proved useful when Tiff and I were in the car — and he suddenly needed to make a note of something that had just occurred to him. All he had to do was reach across, release my pen from its clip, and then replace it when he was done.

My favourite pen was bright orange. One night I wore it to dinner in the Atlantic House. As I was coming downstairs, I saw one of the matrons who regularly sat in a group known to Dorothy Warren as "Stonehenge." The matron was wearing three sets of glasses — one on her eyes, one in her hair and one, like my pen, on a cord around her neck. She stared at me, using each pair in turn, and finally turned to one of her companions and inquired loudly: "Who is that young man wearing a carrot around his neck?"

Not "why," but "who." Lineage — to some — is far more important than motive.

I first discovered this when Tiff and I were invited to a reception given by a prominent Toronto matron in honour of Rudolph Nureyev and Erik Bruhn. We walked up her front steps just behind them. After some delay, our hostess was able to greet us. She expressed her delight in meeting Tiff and, when he introduced me, she mused for a moment and said, "Whitehead? Whitehead? Tell me, who are your people?"

ONCE, WE WERE IN THE DINING room at lunchtime at the Atlantic House when Tiff suddenly froze. He had just spotted, at a table on the other side of the room, Mildred Dunnock. We had been admiring her performances for years. We had a firm policy, though: never interrupt someone else's meal, no matter how intense our admiration might be. And so we waited. And waited. Our table was cleared, and still we sat there. Miss Dunnock dawdled over dessert and coffee, talking with her friends.

Finally, we gave up and went up to our room to change for the afternoon's sojourn on the beach. The phone rang. It was Dorothy Warren. "Tiff, get down here right now! Janet Baldwin has Mildred Dunnock trapped in the parking lot!"

(Janet, a regular visitor to the Atlantic House, was an old family friend of Tiff's, and had once been his dance teacher.)

We found Janet leaning on the open door of Miss Dunnock's car, frantically trying to keep a conversation going. While I hovered nearby, Tiff hurried over and was introduced. Miss Dunnock knew who he was, and had read some of his work. She looked at her watch said, "You know, I'm early for my next appointment, and it's so hot in here. Why don't we go over to the portico and sit in the shade for a while?" Tiff was ecstatic. They sat, while Janet and I ensconced ourselves in chairs on the screened-in porch, which was in earshot just around the corner.

Eventually, their conversation drifted to the subject of Lillian Hellman, in whose plays Tiff knew Miss Dunnock had appeared. There was a sigh, and then she told him how Hellman had been a wonderful writer, but a difficult colleague. She went on to tell a story about rehearsing *Another Part of the Forest*. Lillian suddenly interrupted the proceedings, went over to Miss Dunnock, and remarked that the actress seemed very fond of the scene they were working on. Miss Dunnock tried to express just how much she loved the scene, when Lillian Hellman interrupted her to observe that perhaps the actress liked it *too* much. She then announced that the scene was cut. The play opened without the scene and was presented that way for the entire run.

Eventually, Lillian Hellman sent Miss Dunnock a copy of the printed version. With it was a note; she hoped Miss Dunnock would enjoy having a copy — and also hoped that she would be pleased to see that, in the printed version, the scene Miss Dunnock had loved so much had been restored.

Janet and I heard Miss Dunnock describe to Tiff just how much that bit of cruelty had hurt her. And, with that, she made her goodbyes and left.

There were other notables Tiff and I were to encounter on the beach in Maine. The actor Gary Merrill still owned property near the lighthouse, just down the coast, which he had occupied when he was married to Bette Davis. He would often stroll along the beach with one of several young beauties he apparently knew, always carrying a huge basket, which contained the makings of what seemed like endless martinis. Among his regular guests were friends of ours, so we would be invited to join the party.

Gary was fixated on what he considered to be the unfortunate proclivity of women to wear trousers. As a symbol of his protest, he would often wear a beautifully tailored skirt. Not a kilt, a skirt. We once observed him arrive in the hotel lobby to pick up one of the guests, an extremely elegant woman from Montreal, to take her to dinner. She was making her way down the stairway when she caught sight of him — and of his costume. "Mr. Merrill," she proclaimed, "I cannot be seen with a gentleman wearing a skirt!"

He replied, with a charming smile, "Why not, my dear? It doesn't clash with yours at all."

And then there was Dick Schmidt — a mining engineer, originally from South Africa, married to the daughter of one of the Montreal dynasties who traditionally holidayed there. He has no great claim to fame, except perhaps for sitting on the beach and telling the best shaggy dog story I've ever heard:

There was once a very small and somewhat remote monastery — so small that there were only enough monks for each to be totally responsible for one of the essential tasks in their daily lives.

One day, Brother Bellringer died. There was no one to take his place. For the first time in the history of the place, word was sent out into neighbouring areas that the monastery wished to hire a bell ringer — any bell ringer.

Shortly after, Brother Gatekeeper heard a heavy knocking at the gate. He swung it open and saw, to his astonishment, an armless dwarf who had apparently been using his head to announce his arrival. He was even more astonished at the dwarf's first words.

"Good morning. I have come to apply for the position of bell ringer. Now, I know what you're probably thinking; but I can, indeed, do the job."

The dwarf was taken to the abbot, who was doubtful but kind; he agreed to a demonstration of the little fellow's abilities. They went up into the bell tower, where the dwarf climbed onto a parapet and threw himself headlong at the great bell and smashed, face first, into it. However he had intended to achieve his aim, the bell did indeed begin to sway and ring. The dwarf fell down to the courtyard, where the others, alarmed by the bell, found him dead. They rushed to the abbot, demanding to know what had happened and just who this little man was.

The abbot replied, gravely, "I don't know — but his face certainly rings a bell."

(Significant pause for groans and laughter ...)

The next day.

(Another pause, for astonishment.)

There was more heavy knocking at the gate; lo and behold, another armless dwarf.

"My brother failed miserably, I understand, to be taken on as a bell ringer, so I have come to apply for the job. He and I never did agree on technique."

And so it happened all over again. This time, however, when the dwarf launched himself into space, he did not crash into the bell, but grabbed its rope in his teeth and gave a mighty twist of his head. That, indeed, did set the bell ringing; but, alas, the movement caused the rope to wrap itself around the dwarf's neck and, in a moment, he was swinging, along with the bell, quite dead.

Again, the brothers rushed up to the abbot to discover what had happened and the identity of the man hanging from the rope.

The abbot replied gravely to their question. "I don't know, but he's certainly a dead ringer for his brother."

Words to Die For

*B*y the early 1980s, the lives Tiff and I had created had undergone major changes. I retired from the documentary world. Many people thought it was because of the logistic role I played in Tiff's career — all the support and managerial activities. These did become both more important and, geographically, more diverse as Tiff's popularity spread. They weren't, however, my main reason for ending my day job.

I had always maintained that, whenever possible, the best person to write a documentary script would be the producer/director; that is, the person who had the initial idea and who supervised the shooting of the footage. Nobody else could have the same commitment, the same knowledge and the same intent. Towards the end of my involvement in that world, producers and directors began to take over the role of writer. I would still be offered work, but as a script consultant rather than a script writer. Having been hoist with my own petard, which coincided with the need for more of my time to assist Tiff in his work, I simply stopped writing documentary scripts. It was the right thing to do — and it brought even more happiness into our lives.

Around the same time, we finally woke up to the fact that Christmas celebrations in our home had reached ridiculous proportions. First of all, neither of us was a practising Christian. What were we celebrating? And why? Then there was the cost: we had a Christmas card list of over three hundred and a gift budget in the thousands. What had started out as my baking half-a-dozen coffee cake wreaths for family, friends and neighbours had expanded, over the years, to the production of thirty-six of them — requiring two full days and the assistance of one of the teenagers. I'd wrap each one in foil and store them on the unheated front porch, from where they would be delivered shortly before Christmas for Toronto destinations or on Christmas Eve, locally. I also had to keep careful track of which cakes contained nuts and which did not, because of allergies among our friends.

Then there was Christmas week itself, with every guest room occupied, and three meals a day to prepare. It had become a nightmare — and for what?

We sat down and wrote notes to all our friends and relatives: "We're giving up Christmas. We'll donate our Christmas card money to a charity and, from now on, we ask you to replace Christmas presents with Christmas presence. No gifts, please, but we'd love to see you and join you in a drink."

I think it was the wisest decision we ever made.

SOMETHING ELSE ENTERED OUR LIVES AROUND the same time
— originally with the motive of being merely helpful, though it
proved to be also very wise.

Around that time, the AIDS hospice, Casey House, was
opening. It was one of the many institutions founded by the
astonishing June Callwood, who named it for her son who had
been the fatal victim of a drunk driver. June was a dear friend.
We attended the first big fundraiser for the place, held on
June's sixtieth birthday.

During the party, the film critic Jay Scott dashed over to tell
Tiff that he'd just heard that my first kiss was present, and that
June was about to bring the person over to meet us. I knew
immediately, of course, who it must be — but Tiff had no
idea (I suspect he thought it would be a man). And suddenly
there we were. We hadn't seen each other for over forty years.
It was Margaret McBurney, who — like June — had lost a son
to a drunk-driving accident. She was Margaret McElroy when
I knew her in Regina.

We were eleven or twelve, and it was one of those incredible
Saskatchewan winters; the snow was deep and densely packed.
Margaret and I determined that we would build an igloo —
not, believe me, an easy thing to do. Somehow, though, we
managed it with big knives borrowed from her mother's kitchen
and a hell of a lot of work. When it was finished and we crawled
in to inspect it, we felt that there must be some significant
moment to celebrate the accomplishment. That is when I leaned
over and planted a chaste kiss on Margaret's icy cheek.

How lovely it was to have my past come alive just like that.

When Casey House opened, Tiff and I decided to devote a
day a week to the place as volunteers. As we lived seventy miles

from Toronto, we didn't want to drive all that way for the usual
volunteer shift — three hours — so we arranged to do a double
shift, once a week.

I was asked to handle the telephone switchboard. In order
to understand my reaction to this, you have to go back to my
earliest days.

Hanging on my bedroom wall — along with other artifacts
from my life — is the very first photographic portrait of me ever
taken, in the Regina studios of Wilf West (uncle of Margaret
West, with whom I appeared in a university production of *A
Phoenix Too Frequent*). It was taken in 1934, when I was three.
It is hand-tinted to show little, curly-haired Billy, dressed in his
robin's egg blue knitted suit, long white stockings and patent
leather shoes with buckled straps — lounging on a bench and
talking on the telephone.

Nothing could be more ironic. I hate the telephone. Always
have.

That's why I was so appalled to find that my main task at
Casey House was to sit on the switchboard. What soon con-
quered my resistance to the job was the experience of dealing
with the residents — all of whom were destined to die within
months — and with their families and friends. I had never
before experienced such grace and courage.

As for Tiff, the job was wonderful therapy, among other
things. He had had a lifelong fear of death. By the end of our
two-and-a-half years volunteering at Casey House, most of
that fear was gone. The emotional strength of all those young
men — and of those who loved them — inspired in him a true
sense of reconciliation concerning the end of his own life.

During that period, we occasionally invited the entire staff of the hospice — along with as many of the residents as were capable of making the trip — out to the farm for a swim in the pool and a backyard meal. This is when I learned to cook for fifty or more — great pots of curried shrimp, chicken stew, corn on the cob and tomatoes — all from our garden — served with endless numbers of fruit-topped cream pies and homemade ice cream, which was churned and stored in our giant freezer by our teenage helpers.

In the eighties, travel played an increasing role in our lives. We had always gone on camping trips, but as Tiff's work became more popular we found ourselves spending more and more time away from home, on a seemingly endless series of book tours — all by car or by train, because Tiff refused to fly.

In the fifties, before we met, Tiff had been called to Los Angeles to take on another television writing chore. But, when he got as far as Chicago, it was discovered that his visa (required for US employment) had expired. He thus had to cancel his flight west and spend the night there, to pick up his new visa and then fly the next day. The flight he had originally booked suffered a terrible and fatal accident — a mid-air collision over the Grand Canyon.

It took a fair amount of liquid courage for Tiff to board the next flight, which, happily, made it uneventfully to LA. Unbelievably, disaster struck again. A few days later, an army pilot flew out to take a look at the wreckage in the canyon — and hit another commercial plane.

Tiff swore he would never fly again. And so, I did a lot of driving.

One of our drives was a once-in-a-lifetime event. We won first prize in a Cannington raffle. The prize: a trip, by air, to the great Disney World in Florida. Lovely — but neither of us wanted to romp around with Mickey Mouse, and there seemed to be no way to persuade Tiff to board a plane.

So we made a deal. If we drove down at our own expense, could the prize be a stay on one of those lovely little islands off the Gulf Coast — Sanibel or Captiva? The deal was accepted; and, since we were allowed a guest, we invited my old friend and Tiff's researcher, Beverley Roberts.

All was well once we got there, but the trip down was hell. If I may offer this advice: do not travel with a researcher.

Beverley had armed herself with just about every known fact on the subject of everything we passed on the way — and she read aloud from her notes, all the way down.

Finally we reached Fort Myers, from which a causeway led to the islands. I was amazed. For one thing, the town had grown immeasurably since Herb Foster and I had camped on its empty beaches during our circumnavigation of the US in 1959. And, for another, the road that led us to our luxury hotel passed through the most rundown slum I had ever seen. It reminded me of some of the native communities Tiff and I had seen in the Northwest Territories in 1969: abject poverty, except for the elegant church and equally elegant manse.

The hotel was great. The food was great. The beach was terrific. Oddly, we were the only guests on it. Everybody else was crowded around the swimming pool, with one woman bitching at the top of her lungs that the water was advertised to be kept at eighty degrees and was only seventy-five.

We kept our eyes on her, and sneered inwardly at her gold lamé bathing suit, her stiletto heels and her interminable dissatisfactions. Aha, we thought. Typically American. (As was the fact all our "servants" were African-American — maids, waitresses, busboys, pool attendants and gardeners; all, we discovered, bussed in daily from that dreadful slum we had passed.) But we had to stop sneering. We saw her, one day, get into her car and drive off. Her car had Ontario licence plates.

IT WAS ON THAT FLORIDA TRIP that I first heard a person utter the ubiquitous southern phrase: "Y'all come back now, ya hear!" I swear that some of our starlings at the farm had picked it up when they spent their winters in the south. Starlings, like mynah birds, are pretty good mimics.

Once Tiff started setting extra dog chow outside the dogs' pen to feed the three crows that traditionally stayed with us all winter, our flock of about fifty starlings no longer flew south. They simply roosted in our winter-barren trees, waiting for their daily lunch.

In the eighties, shortly before Tiff started work on his next novel, there was a significant — and, for me, welcome — change in our lives. It began with an invitation from Vancouver for Tiff to give a major lecture — for a decidedly major fee. There was only one problem. With all our other commitments, the only way to get to Vancouver on time was to fly — and this, Tiff was still unwilling to do.

Now, although he was president of the company the two of us had founded in the late seventies — Pebble Productions, Inc. — I was treasurer. The treasurer had a little word with the president.

"You can do this," I told him. I would arrange a lovely hotel room at the airport for the night before the flight. A hired limo would get us there, where some very good wines would await us in the room and at dinner. It could also be arranged with Tiff's psychiatrist that a slightly more generous supply of tranquilizers be made available for the flight.

Tiff reluctantly agreed to try. What he discovered, thank goodness, was that in the thirty years since he had last been on a plane, air travel had greatly changed for the better.

Flying made our travels much easier and faster — and so much more pleasant.

I think it's safe to say that starting in the eighties, most of our travels were book tours — the promotional activity most publishers demand of most writers.

Most book tours skip Newfoundland. It takes time and expense to get there, and the perception was that the province's readership is not large. I can't speak about the costs or the number of readers, but I certainly can attest to their enthusiasm — and to the utter charm of the Newfoundland accent.

On one visit to St. John's, an interview with Tiff was filmed, which was to be used at a later event in Toronto. The Hotel Newfoundland kindly let us use one of their private dining rooms for the shoot, during which a waitress from the public dining room appeared with very welcome coffee for us all. She took in what was going on and left.

When we broke for lunch, it was she who served us. The person she addressed was Tiff. Under the impression that all the equipment was for a photographic portrait, she asked, "So, me darlin' — didja say 'cheese' or 'Pehhhpsi'?"

Winnipeg also often had something memorable to offer us. One year, Tiff was slated for a television interview following one with Mary Shaver, whose autobiographical book, *The Naked Nun*, was a bit of a sensation that year. She had been kicked out of the order for posing nude for her art class.

The interviewer, we discovered, was a nervous young man who acted as if this were his first time conducting an interview. He smiled uncertainly at Miss Shaver, picked up her book, and discovered that it had two front covers. The first showed the author in full habit; the second showed her as she had posed for her class. He stared at the second picture for a moment, terrified, and then turned to look at Tiff, who was still off camera. "Uhh … Mr. Findley? Why don't … I mean … won't you join us … now?" Tiff obliged, whereupon the young neophyte stammered, "I was w-w-wondering … I mean … given your age and all … and your experience … what would you ask the n-n-naked n-n-nun?"

And those were the last words he uttered for the course of the program; Tiff and Mary had a lively and pleasant talk.

EVENTUALLY THESE TOURS INCLUDED EUROPEAN COUNTRIES — Germany and especially France, where Tiff was extremely popular.

For part of our first German tour, the publisher herself accompanied us. She was a beautiful and surprisingly young creature named Doris Janhsen. When Tiff began having problems wrestling with his luggage and managing the distances between our part of the train and the station, we began to mutter about the "myth of German efficiency." Doris gave no sign that she had heard, but simply began enthusing about the unique hotel we would occupy that night. It had once been a monastery, she said, but was now completely renovated, featuring the very latest in German hotel technology.

She saw us in through the front doors, and then went off to

her own hotel, where some sort of a meeting had been arranged.

We went to the desk.

It was extraordinary. The desk clerk was seated high above us, rather like a judge in a courtroom. Registration was definitely low-tech. Just the usual stuff. Then he gave us a key card and pointed out the elevator. So far, so good.

We reached our floor, left the elevator and headed down the hall.

Halfway down, the lights went out.

I told Tiff to sit on his largest suitcase; I'd be right back. Then I felt my way to the elevator, and eventually made it all the way to the desk.

"The lights went out," I said.

"They're on a timer," the clerk explained.

"I gather that, but the time's too short."

"It's been determined by experts," he said. "You have to walk faster."

"Do you have a flashlight?" I asked.

Amazingly, he did — and let me borrow it.

I went back up to Tiff. We found our door. I inserted the key card and tried the knob. Nothing happened. I tried several times more — in several ways. Nothing.

I told Tiff to sit on the same suitcase and returned to the desk.

"The key card doesn't work," I said.

"Yes it does," he replied. "If you use it correctly."

"And what is 'correctly'?" I asked.

I swear this was his answer: "You put the card only one-third of the way in. Then you turn the door handle ninety degrees to the right. Another third of the way, turn one-hundred-and-eighty degrees to the left. Put the card all the way in, return the handle to the upright position. The door will open."

I stared at him for a moment, and then returned to Tiff. I followed the instructions. The door opened.

I won't go through the whole routine, but ... Once we got into the room, the lights wouldn't go on. Further trips revealed that the key card had to be inserted into a slot in the wall before the switches would respond. And — wouldn't you know it — the television only worked once we discovered its key slot, but we had to leave the card in the slot while we watched, because we would be charged according to how long we watched.

In the morning, when Doris picked us up to help us catch the next train, we had a fair amount to say about "German efficiency." She simply smiled.

When we reached the station, we were met by two strong young men driving a large baggage cart — with seats for passengers. We were taken, baggage and all, directly to our car's door. The two young men stowed our luggage in the racks above and below our seats.

As we sank gratefully into our places, Doris took out the manuscript she intended to read on the way and observed, as she opened it at page one: "I think we've heard enough about German efficiency." She gave us one of her lovely smiles.

THE NEXT SERIES OF FLIGHTS TIFF was persuaded to make took us all the way to Australia, to attend the Adelaide Literary Festival and Canada Week in Sydney.

We flew first to Hawaii and then on to Sydney. The second flight lasted fifteen hours and Tiff grew very nervous when he noticed that the plane's engines were causing enough vibration to loosen the screws in the ceiling above us. As we watched them drop to the floor, a flight attendant came by, took in the situation and soon reappeared with a bottle of wine. He handed it to Tiff with one quiet comment: "Here. I think this might help."

We landed at Sydney and had time for a quick cigarette outside before moving on to Adelaide. The first whiff of the air was exhilarating. Tiff turned to me and said: "You know? I've never breathed such clean air. Not a whiff of North America!"

From Adelaide, we were whisked away up into the hills to recover from our long flight in a lovely little cabin. While I unpacked, Tiff went into his habitual retreat, the bathroom. Soon, there was a knock at the back door. I opened it to discover a very large lady in a pink uniform, clutching a handful of flowers.

"Allo, dear. Just come to do up your flies."

I heard the bathroom lock go snick.

In the next moment, as she started arranging the bouquet in a vase on the table, I realized that "flies" was Australian for "flowers."

Later, listening to the radio, we heard a male chorus sing a rousing recruitment song for the reserve army. The opening lyrics went something like this: "Come on, guys. Join us. We got the energy. We got the expertise. We got the Antichrist."

Antichrist? It took two more listens to decipher "enterprise."

We were delighted, at the festival in Adelaide, to renew acquaintances with a young Australian woman whom Tiff had befriended when he was writer-in-residence at the University of Toronto. We arranged to have lunch with her the following day, along with, "if we didn't mind," her new husband, whom she didn't name.

It turned out she had married Peter Carey, who had just won the Booker Prize for *Oscar and Lucinda*.

Tiff never got to give his reading in Adelaide. Whatever the pressures, he disappeared for a week. All I could do was notify the festival officials and wait as patiently as I could in the hotel room. Eventually, Tiff returned. And eventually he was contrite for giving in, once again, to alcohol. Fortunately, when we met some of the festival organizers a few years later — this time during a visit to Perth, on the west coast — there was no evidence that they even remembered this earlier disaster.

On that first trip, we also went to Sydney. Most of our reasons for being there did not come to fruition — thanks to mismanagement at the Canadian Consulate, Tiff did get to give a reading. It took place at a pub near the dog racing tracks.

The pub had two huge rooms. The outer one was filled with very noisy people having a terrifically good time. The inner one had a slightly raised platform for the reader, with a sawdust-strewn floor where scores of young people were sitting and standing, drinking and eagerly awaiting the readings.

The first reading was by Thomas Keneally, whose novel *Schindler's Ark*, also the winner of the Booker Prize, became the basis of Spielberg's film *Schindler's List* — although he didn't receive much credit for it. The next reader was the American, Ken Kesey — a delightful man and as good a reader as he was a writer.

Shortly after Ken started in, there was a tremendous crash in the next room, followed by yells, screams and, ultimately, sirens. Ken glanced up, shrugged and continued reading. It wasn't until he and the applause had finished that we discovered what had happened. A fight had broken out, with one combatant tossing the other right out into the street — through one of the huge windows that fronted the bar. When we all finally left, people were still cleaning up the glass and the blood. Thankfully, there had been no dire injuries.

WHILE ACCENTS PRESENT THEIR OWN DANGERS, perhaps the most subtle trap of all is formed by words that usually have one shade of meaning but can have others. A highly embarrassing example of this became apparent at a social event in Vancouver, held at what I call "The Hanging Gardens of Babylon" because of its cascading, plant-laden terraces — better known as Vancouver's Courthouse. The occasion was a dinner arranged in honour of the wonderful Ken Dryden — to honour his time and effort fostering hockey as a means of improving the lives of the young, especially young men.

After drinks and a pleasant meal, an older man with a mild face got up and went to the microphone.

"Ladies and gentlemen," he began. "I have something to tell you about Ken Dryden." He beamed a smile all around. "Ken Dryden … loves boys!"

A nervous silence fell over the room.

"Yes, Ken Dryden loves boys. And Ken Dryden knows what boys love. And furthermore Ken Dryden knows how to give boys exactly what they love!"

The silence was broken by a few muted giggles. Of course, we all knew that the other implication that lay in those words was utterly inappropriate. Unfortunately, it was just that knowledge that made the words so irresistibly funny.

I tried to hide my reddening face behind my napkin, but by then my whole body was shaking. I looked up, and saw others at my table having the same problem. They included several representatives of Penguin Canada — Tiff's publishers — as well as the head librarian at the University of British Columbia.

Soon, the all-too-evident suppression of mirth spread to another table, then another, until the whole room was in silent convulsions. Silent, yes, all too evidently — except to the speaker. He smiled his way through the rest of his address.

What we all saw in Ken Dryden, when he approached the microphone to respond to those remarks, was the bravest and most tactful man imaginable. He gave a simple thanks for the honour the speaker's words had meant to convey, and launched into his own speech — which was graceful, informative and interesting. Afterwards, he mingled and eventually we all went home. Some of us chastened.

Somewhat related to naïvety is the literal mind. William Hutt used to tell a story that beautifully illustrates this.

A postman was about to retire and felt a little sad about it. He cheered up, though, when he reached his favourite house, with its huge, gorgeous brass mailbox. He was about to complete his delivery when the front door was opened by a quite lovely young woman.

"Hello," she said. "Won't you come in?" She took him by the hand, led him down a hall to a dining room where the table was set for two: Spode china, Georgian silverware and Waterford crystal — four glasses at each setting.

An incredible meal was served. There was conversation, and after coffee the woman rose and said: "Now — won't you come upstairs?"

She led the way to a bedroom where, for over an hour, the two enjoyed mind-blowing sex.

Once they were dressed, the postman began to zombie his way down the stairs, followed by the woman — who suddenly stopped. "Oh, silly me — I almost forgot!" She dashed back to the bedroom. In a moment she appeared with her purse, from which she extracted a five-dollar bill.

"Here," she said with a smile. "This is for you."

The postman, completely puzzled, slowly took the bill.

"Well, I guess I should explain," the woman said. "You see, I knew this was your last day. I heard about it at the supermarket. Last night, when my husband got home from the office, I told him and asked him if we shouldn't do something? And he said: 'Fuck him. Give him five dollars.' Lunch was my idea!"

Hutt always told the punch line in one go. I usually pause before the final sentence, to get two laughs.

AS EVERY SUCCESSFUL WRITER KNOWS, HE is expected to do much more than just write the words. He must also help to sell them. This means weeks on the road, or on the water or in the air — living in hotels, rushing from interview to interview, often sacrificing lunch or — even worse — trying to answer an interviewer's questions while also trying to take in some food.

The worst book tour for Tiff was in 1990, for *Inside Memory*. Nine solid weeks, with only one day free of travel or publicity work. Tiff had to go to an emergency ward in Halifax to deal with exhaustion and the flu. By the time we reached Vancouver, he was again close to collapse. At that emergency ward, the doctor — seeing me — suspected AIDS. While the blood test was being analyzed, he directed us to stand by in the waiting room. When he appeared, he looked grimly at Tiff — and suggested that it might be a good idea if I came along as well. This immediately signalled to us that what we were about to hear was dire.

It wasn't. The results of the test were negative. Tiff could see that I was ready to explode with accusations centring on "Then why the hell did your attitude imply the reverse!" And he hurried us out of the room.

I began to wonder, though — were Tiff's beloved words slowly killing him?

In 1994, we both felt that a long, relaxing holiday was absolutely necessary. Tiff had finished *Headhunter* — the book tour would be that fall — and was well into *The Piano Man's Daughter*, which was slated to come out the following year. Having just received a goodly sum for a batch of Findley archives, we decided to visit Florence, Athens and a couple of Greek islands, ending up in Provence where we had arranged to rent a small house for a month with the assistance of Marigold Charlesworth. The house was owned by a British couple named Ashdown. Mrs. Ashdown had been Marigold's schoolgirl friend.

We rented a car at the airport in Nice, intending to drive for about an hour in order to meet Marigold and Jean Roberts at their own house, which was less than an hour from Cotignac, the village where our rental was located. We were early, so we decided to stop for something to eat — and that's when I discovered something that I understand many North Americans have discovered to their sorrow. The only way I could get out of our parking space was to back out, but I couldn't get the car into reverse. There's a trick to it in France. The proper position of the gear shift is plainly marked on the shift's knob, but you have to know that, in order to get it into that position, your fingers have to lift a tiny lever on the shaft.

Fortunately, there was a service station right next door; the attendant laughingly explained what I had to do.

Success! After we met our friends, we drove to our house — Marigold taking Tiff in their car, Jean driving me in ours. Given the twisting and complex set of roadways in Provence, this was definitely the smartest way for us to go the first time.

We didn't know it, but Cotignac nestles at the foot of a towering red stone cliff — known either as a *rocher* or a *falaise*, depending on who tells you (some argue that a *falaise* properly names only a cliff that rises out of water). The road arrives at the top of the cliff — the village is in a deep valley — and then twists down with stunning views of the whole place. We drove along a side road for a short distance — and there was the house, a charming bungalow on a property that cascaded down the valley side in several stages, with the house on the second terrace down.

The gardens were vibrant with flowering shrubs, iris, oleander, cypress and olive trees — with thyme and rosemary growing wild all around. Heaven!

We went into the *cours* for lunch under huge plane trees. And, before we knew it, Tiff and I were alone in the house we would occupy for a month — each with our own bedroom and bath, a well-equipped kitchen and that gorgeous garden.

We were so enchanted with the place that, when we got home, I asked the owners if we might stay in it again the following year.

Tiff was childlike in his love of surprises. That's why I didn't tell him that I'd also asked the owners to let us know if they ever wanted to sell the place. I received a call from them one evening, back in Cannington, while we were cooking dinner.

After I hung up I told Tiff who had called, and asked, "Do you want the good news or the bad?"

He excitedly chose the good. I told him that, indeed, we could rent the place again. And then I said: "The bad news is it's just been sold."

He was devastated — so I finished my sentence.

"To us."

I don't remember exactly what he was holding at that moment, but whatever it was left a dent in the kitchen ceiling that was still there when we ultimately sold Stone Orchard.

The following summer we eagerly took possession of the place, fully furnished. There were even some books that had been left behind.

One of the first things Tiff did, of course, was to go through the books to see what he would like to keep. I was in the kitchen when I heard him give a yell. He appeared with one of the books in his hand, a look of utter amazement on his face.

The book was *Stendhal on Love*, and the flyleaf bore the handwritten name: Maruja Duncan.

I recognized the name. Maruja was the daughter of Jimmy Duncan who, as a young man, had worked at Massey-Harris when Tiff's grandfather, Thomas Findley, was its president. Jimmy Duncan was, in fact, the man who had located Uncle Tif, badly wounded in a Belgian field hospital. Jimmy had married a Spanish actress — Trina — hence the Spanish name of their daughter.

It seemed that our second home was to offer the same kind of family roots that Stone Orchard had given us. My stepfather's grandfather had been an innkeeper just a few minutes away. More evidence of what a small world this is.

But how, we wondered, had that book found its way to Provence?

We learned from Marigold that Dr. Ashdown had lived in the Bahamas, which is where Maruja had grown up. We mailed the book back to her, care of her husband's office. Her husband is Hal Jackman, who had gone to school with Tiff and was then Lieutenant Governor of Ontario.

ONE OF THE FIRST IMPROVEMENTS WE made to our new home was to create a writing studio for Tiff. We had inherited the Ashdowns' multitalented handyman — an Englishman named John Bertram. We asked him to create the studio out of the garage situated at the top of the valley side property. It was completed in time for a shipment of our Canadian belongings, including all of Tiff's working library, along with his treasured office furniture (hand-crafted by our Canadian handyman, Len Collins) and his favourite artworks and dolls — a series of human, animal and mythical figures he had collected over the years.

That was in 1995. For the rest of Tiff's life, we would spend half of each year in Cotignac — beyond the reach of most of the many who wanted some part of Tiff's attention and time.

It was a highly productive time for him; but, for us both, it was also a constant struggle to live in another language. Tiff spoke no French at all, and what little I knew of the language had been gained at school, over forty years earlier.

It's not surprising, then, that we had so many misadventures with the language. For a long time, Tiff would insist that I accompany him whenever he had to negotiate even the simplest task in French. One day, he announced that he was going to walk down into the centre of the village and get a haircut. He

had, he assured me, established the words he would need —
and he promised to rehearse them all the way to *la coiffeuse*.
He eventually made it home — nicely shorn. I asked him how
it had gone. He looked a bit sheepish. "All the way down, I
rehearsed '*Bonjour, madame, voulez-vous couper mes cheveux.*'
But by the time I got there, it had morphed into '*Voulez-vous
écouter mes chevaux.*'" ("Would you listen to my horses.")

Madame had been very sweet. With a big smile, she looked
out into the street and said, in French, "Willingly, Monsieur,
where are your horses?"

Similar blunders on my part were a bit more dangerous.

Tiff's work was very popular in France, having been translated into French. He was ultimately made a *Chevalier de
l'Ordre des Arts et des Lettres*, with a lovely ceremony in Paris
at which the Minister of Culture received him into the order.
Afterwards, the minister hosted a celebratory luncheon in
a grand building nearby — at a huge round table with other
dignitaries and some of our friends. We were deeply grateful
that acknowledgement was made of our weaknesses in French;
the entire meal was conducted in English. At one point, I muttered to Tiff that we would need to express our gratitude for
this in French. He muttered back, "Yes. Go ahead."

I worked up what I thought might be a suitably gracious
sentence. As I wasn't confident about my tenses, I slipped
around the table to consult with one of the Canadian journalists
at that moment in the meal when there's a break for everyone
to circulate and greet friends. When I whispered my gracious
sentence, he collapsed into laughter.

Apparently, I was about to say to the Minister of Culture:
"Minister, Timothy Findley and I want to express our deep

gratitude for this magnificent meal — and for the kindness you and your wife have shown in so graciously acknowledging our deficiencies in your beautiful language. Please accept our thanks — and also, if you would, grant us permission to have sex with your charming wife."

Now, when I had learned French, *baiser* meant "to kiss." As a noun, it still means a kiss — but the verb has evolved into something much more forceful and more frequently encountered in the gutter than in gentle society. These linguistic evolutions occur in English, too. In my teens, there was a standard question any guy might ask of another guy who had taken a girl out: "How'd you make out?" Meaning: "How far did you get?" Now, as I understand it, "making out" is roughly equivalent to what we called "necking" — embraces involving kissing.

During our stays in Cotignac, I learned to speak enough French to get by; enough to shop in French, dine in French and even spend five-hour meals with Francophone friends — as long as they were patient with me. My problem was that I had tremendous difficulty in understanding spoken French, especially since I was partly deaf in my right ear. My standard apology was: "*Excusez-moi, mais je suis un peu sourd — et, malheureusement, j'ai encore les oreilles anglaises.*" ("I'm a bit deaf, and I still have English ears.")

It took me as long in French as it had in English to learn the rougher elements of a sexual vocabulary. After I had mastered some of the French slang for body parts and sexual activity, I asked a local restaurateur to tell me the dirtiest French word of all. He did, and I stored it away, noting its similarity to another word I already knew.

And therein lay my perennial problem — trying to distinguish which word meant what.

A time came when we had more books shipped over from Canada. We received a call that the truck was on its way. The driveway leading from the upper road down to the house was not only steep, it curved. During the call, I forgot to tell the driver to be sure to back down the driveway, since going backwards up the slope would be decidedly difficult. Because of this oversight, I stationed myself at the foot of the drive and waited. I waited for about half an hour — and then had to make a lightning visit to the bathroom. When I returned, there was the truck, coming down the roadway front-first. I ran up, waving my arms and shouting.

"*Non, non, monsieur, Enculez! Enculez!*" The words had scarcely left my mouth when I realized I should have used another one — *reculez*, which means "back up." It was no wonder the driver looked shocked and puzzled. I was pelting up towards him, exhorting him, loudly and explicitly, to submit to anal sex.

ALL KINDS OF DANGER LURKS IN the use of words from other languages. It's so easy to confuse two words with similar sounds but wildly different meanings. My favourite example is probably apocryphal; it's a story about three immigrant construction workers discussing the fact that their foreman had just discovered that his wife was unable to have children. "Yes," declared one, "she is inconceivable." "No," said the next. "You mean impregnable." The third piped up, triumphantly: "Idiots! She is unbearable!"

It happens even within one's own language. Consider the different sentiments expressed by two apparently similar declarations: "When I look at you, time stands still," and "You've got a face that would stop a clock!"

ONE OF THE HIGHLIGHTS OF ANY winter stay at Cotignac was the annual New Year's visit to Tiff's agent, Bruce Westwood, who had a house near Nice where he traditionally spent a few weeks each year.

It was a lovely place, in a gated community that occupied a hill beside the one that featured the famous hill village of St-Paul-de-Vence. The only building on Bruce's property when he bought it was an old shepherd's hut. He then hired a team of North African stonemasons to quarry stone from the property's outcroppings and, with the help of an architect, build a magnificent house and swimming pool. He converted the hut into a guest cottage, which is where Tiff and I would stay.

On one visit, a literary agent from Britain was a fellow guest. The three of us decided to walk down the hill and make a dinner reservation at the famous restaurant just outside the gates of St-Paul — roughly across the street from what was once James Baldwin's studio. It was in an equally famous hotel, which featured a Calder mobile beside the swimming pool — and, as we discovered, Miro originals on some of the bedroom walls.

After making our reservation, we paused on a convenient bench overlooking the restaurant before tackling the steep road back to Bruce's house. As we sat there, one of the longest limousines I've ever seen drew up to the restaurant and about a dozen young men poured out. They all had black hair and wore black suits. They looked Italian, and I wondered out loud if it might be some Italian dignitary or superstar. The agent glanced

down, laughed and said, "No, it's the little chap in the bad wig."
I looked again and saw it was Elton John.

ONE OF THE BEST THINGS ABOUT spending time in France was
having access to that wonder of the culinary world, the truffle.

About half an hour away, there was a town with an annual
truffle market. Although there was an indoor market, carefully
scrutinized by police, there was a black market of salesmen
wandering around — equally carefully ignored by the police.
The wandering salesmen behaved in much the same way as the
men I had once encountered in Ciudad Juarez, that dreadful
Mexican border town famous for its drug and pornography
trade. There, you couldn't avoid seedy-looking characters who
would sidle up, flash open their jackets and reveal different
collections of "feelthy peectures." Here, the wares were truffles.
You could covertly fondle and sniff a sample; and then, if interested, follow the vendor to some back street where his car was
parked. In the trunk was a supply of those extraordinary fungi
— at extraordinary prices: low at the beginning of the season,
but growing higher as the weeks passed and the supply dwin-
dled. Low, to my initial horror, was roughly the equivalent of
one hundred dollars a pound. The highest I ever encountered
was almost four times that amount.

Another boon for us was the abundance and variety of local
olives. Our own garden contained several olive trees. At first
we felt we didn't have time to harvest them, and we certainly
believed we would never tackle processing them, however much
we cherished the idea of using our own olive oil. But then
John Bertram offered to help us pick them. The local *coopératif*
not only made wine for owners of small vineyards, who could

simply bring their harvest to the place, but also made olive oil for people with a relatively small number of olive trees. All we had to do in order to enjoy this privilege was to join.

One day I stopped in to talk to the lady in charge of such matters. She treated me quite dismissively. "Only eighteen trees? Oh, monsieur. I don't think so. Not even if you followed procedure and wrote a letter to the director. He is dreadfully busy, and probably won't have time to reply."

At first I was discouraged. Then, I remembered something I had read in a book a friend had given me: *French — or Foe*. It had been written by an American, as an aid to US executives working in France, and it offered endless hints about how to deal with this foreign culture.

I had been intrigued by the chapter "The Nine Magic Words," and suddenly realized that this was the perfect opportunity to try them out. And so I put on my most forlorn face and declared: "*Excusez-moi, madame, de vous deranger — mais, j'ai une probleme.*" Forgive me for disturbing you, madam, but I have a problem.

This was meant to provide madame (or monsieur) with an immediate feeling of power and superiority, and to encourage the provision of some kind of help for this unfortunate foreigner.

Madame looked at me sharply and asked "Une probleme? Quoi?"

My what, I hinted, was that I was quite unequipped to write a letter of any kind, let alone one gracious and effective enough to receive a positive reply. I somehow must have managed to squeeze all of that into one word — "Moi?" — uttered in the most helpless tones I could muster, because she suddenly snorted, turned to her typewriter and banged out a few lines, had me sign them, took my cheque, disappeared into a nearby office and reappeared almost immediately with papers that declared my membership in the co-op.

Magic words, indeed!

Unfortunately, we never did get around to an olive harvest. Work multiplied, as did several other problems.

WITHIN A COUPLE OF YEARS WE came to a sad realization: with so much time spent in France — and on book tours across Canada, France, Germany and a few cities in the US — Stone Orchard, in practical terms, no longer had a viable place in our lives. It was an extremely difficult decision to reach. It was devastating for Tiff. He had spent years with the comforting thought that when he died he would be in a place he loved with all his beloved cats and dogs.

And so Stone Orchard was put up for sale, unbelievably to many. That meant finding someone to occupy the house — and someone else to look after the cats and the gardens. With the help of the local veterinarians, Debbie Davies and Mike Stephenson, the two dogs, Casey and Minnie, were placed in a new farm home. Debbie also found a housesitter — a young local who was helping his parents run their family farm, but wanted to live on his own. Len Collins still supervised the care of the gardens.

It took years to find a buyer, which was all to the good, because it took us a long time to settle on another Canadian base. At first, we thought of the town of Guelph — with its wonderful bookstore, the Bookshelf, and plenty of our friends. We began quietly to look for a condo, but soon that came to an abrupt stop the evening we attended a dinner party that included several faculty members from the University of Guelph. When we let it be known we were thinking of moving to Guelph, there was universal acclaim: Tiff would be available to give readings and workshops, he could be a guest lecturer.

No. That would truly be a case of out of the frying pan and into the fire.

It was Tiff who finally said, "What the hell's the matter with us? It's obvious where we should go. Stratford! Plenty of theatre — and no university!"

We started looking in Stratford for a condo large enough to offer each of us a bedroom — and each an office. The search seemed a total failure, until we got a call from an acquaintance who was involved in the conversion of an old apartment building into six modern condos and two restaurants.

We went to inspect it and were a little startled that it was situated right on the main street, in the centre of the business section. We talked to the architect. The possibilities were glorious. We could bargain for a bit more space than was originally planned for the suite — and we could plan all the details of the interior design.

The price was settled, the contract signed. Back we went to France.

I had made up what we called "the decorator's bible." It outlined in detail what was to be done, and offered samples of paint colours, wallpaper, tile designs, carpeting … everything. We left it with the contractor, who could have his workers follow it while we were away.

Over the next few months I began to receive overseas calls from Stratford. It was the contractor. The calls pretty well amounted to this: "Uh, Bill." (Laugh.) "I've been talking to Mike, the painter. Now ... it isn't that he doesn't like your colours. He loves 'em! But ... you know, he's used to doing off-white and ivory and stuff, and so ... he's asked me to check ... just one more time. Do you really want *all sixteen* of those pretty *vivid* colours?"

Each time, my reply was the same: "Yes, please." I understood the problem. I had keyed all the colours to the two William Morris wallpapers we had chosen, and since all the painting was being done before the wallpaper went up, I guess the colours did look a little startling. By the time it was all done, though, even the contractor was happy.

We first saw the finished place in the spring of 1999.

The last time we had seen it was before construction had begun, when it was a vast barnlike space on the second floor, stretching from the front — which overlooked the town's main business intersection — all the way to the back, which lay on a little cobblestoned laneway. It was a dark and cavernous space, with a few dead pigeons on the floor.

The condo we walked into was a fully built and decorated wonder. It would be perfect once all our stored furniture and belongings arrived. Even today, after living here for almost twelve years, I can't enter the place without pausing to take it all in.

The building contains six units spread over two floors. Our place was one of only two units occupied by the owners. The other owners visit occasionally, but rent their apartments to a series of Stratford Festival visitors.

One morning, shortly after we moved in, I was at my computer and Tiff was at the other end of the apartment in his bathroom, as usual. Suddenly, I heard an extraordinary voice in the hall right outside my study door. "Oh, the colours! Look at the colours!"

I rose and walked into the hall to discover two little old ladies, one with short, bright yellow hair — and a deep whiskey voice. She spoke to me.

"I hope you don't mind, but we're staying just across the hall and we've heard about this place, and we're simply dying to have a look at it. Would that be possible?"

I was so dumbfounded that I simply nodded. After all, Tiff was safely tucked away, and would not emerge for some time. What harm could they do?

I went back to work, hearing a series of exclamations in the distance: "Oh, the drapes! Look at the drapes! And these little shelves in the hall. That's what you need, dear!" And so on. And then complete silence. What on earth were they doing now? And where were they?

I knew where they were and would deal with it.

I hurried down the hall to Tiff's area and found them exactly where I expected, standing just inside his study, gazing up at something on the wall.

It was a large pencil drawing by Claire Weissman Wilks, from her erotic series. It showed the torsos of two male nudes in full erection.

My little deep-voiced friend saw me and uttered the impossible. "Oh, good. You're here. Do you have a ruler?"

I was speechless.

As in Australia, I heard the bathroom lock go snick. Before I could recover, the little visitor explained. "You see, my friend here can't see the second penis, and I thought that if I had a ruler I could point it out to her."

I smiled weakly, found the ruler on the desk across the room and pointed to what I presumed was the second penis.

They both nodded, and looked pleased.

And then they left.

I found out, afterwards, that the silent visitor was a Mrs. Goodman, from the theatre family in Chicago. Her bizarre companion was her maid.

Later, Tiff asked me how I had determined which was the second penis.

"Tiffy," I assured him. "If two penises are involved, I always know whose the second is."

ALL WE NEEDED NOW WAS TO sell Stone Orchard. Many had come to inspect it, but there were no takers until one of Toronto's most elegant women — the realtor, Sis Weld — took over and sold the place to the ballet star Rex Harrington. It all happened just in time to allow us to pay for our new place.

Sadly, other changes — far less welcome — were beginning to enter our lives.

Tiff's astonishing productivity began to take its toll. His energy level dropped. He began to fall victim to the hereditary weaknesses of the Findleys: bad legs and bad lungs. Early in 2002, we planned a sojourn in France; he needed a good rest before beginning two projects, an adaptation of *The Trojan Women* for Stratford's 2003 season, and a new novel.

Instead of boarding a plane, however, he went into intensive care in Stratford, with pulmonary failure.

By the end of March, he was declared fit. Off to France we flew.

The first week in Cotignac was terrific as we experienced

total relaxation. Then, the night before Tiff was planning to start work on the play, he took a midnight fall onto the tile floor of his bathroom.

He called out to me in the morning. I called Cotignac's doctor, who confirmed my suspicion. Tiff had a fractured pelvis. An ambulance was summoned to take him to the hospital in Brignoles, about twenty kilometres away. I followed him to the hospital, saw him settled in and went off to buy him a small bottle of wine. Happily, French hospitals allow this.

My greatest worry concerned Tiff's tranquilizers. His Toronto doctor had warned him that over the years he had acquired a prescribed addiction to them. It would be dangerous to his mental health if he ever tried to stop taking them. I took a supply to the hospital, explained the situation and was sent home with a scolding. How dare I interfere with professional care of a patient? A few days later I was asked to bring the pills back.

A week later, Tiff was allowed to come home, where he stayed for only a week. He was disoriented, not interested in food or drink and in constant pain. A local nurse came every day, but his condition declined. The pain worsened. He looked terrible. He was taken back to Brignoles, from where he was transferred to an excellent military hospital in Toulon. (This was accomplished with the help of the Canadian Embassy in Paris, alerted by our old friend Adrienne Clarkson, then Governor General.) I saw Tiff for a few minutes before he was taken into intensive care. That is the last time I was sure he was able to see me.

For the next two months, I drove to Toulon every other day. I would put on a gown and a mask to spend a few minutes speaking to Tiff, with no sign he could hear me.

Finally, around 1:30 in the early morning of June 21, 2002, I got the call. *Il est decedé.* Deceased.

A brief service at the crematorium was held a few days later. The assemblage small: Jean and Marigold, then living in France, a couple of neighbours and a few other friends. We were ten.

Afterward, we had lunch at a restaurant run by a couple who attended the service. Then I went home.

That was when it struck me. I would never see Tiff again.

We had been together just over forty years; to be honest, I don't think I will ever deal completely with his absence. Our lives — both personal and professional — had been too closely intertwined to allow just one of those lives to continue on with comfort or confidence.

I felt as if I were sleepwalking my way through the next year and a half. There were memorials to attend or help put together — in Stratford, Toronto and Paris. There was Pebble Productions Inc. to run, which held copyright to all of Tiff's works. There was the Stratford condo to occupy and manage. And there was the house in Cotignac to sell.

I tried staying there alone, but that simply didn't work. I tried having friends and relatives over for visits, but that didn't help matters, either — even though it gave me plenty to do. In 2003, I put the house on the market.

I made a few other trips with friends: spending Christmas in the Caribbean's St. Vincent and the Grenadines, to the island of Bequia with my film director friend Terry Filgate and his wife, Lorna. It was mildly pleasant, but I'm no water baby — and not as social as Terry and Lorna. A holiday means a quiet time in a pleasant place. Their friends were all scuba divers, and while we might start out our stay there with just the three of us at table, by the time we left the island we might be as many as twelve.

I made a trip to Italy with an old friend, Jane Rowland, who had been Tiff's publicist at HarperCollins. We visited Venice, and then went to the Tuscan village of Pienza, whose beautiful church is featured in the film of *The English Patient*.

I returned from that very pleasant voyage with what turned out to be a misleadingly startling revelation. I was merely having fun when I announced to friends that while in Tuscany I had lost part of my virginity. Undaunted by the somewhat nervous reaction to this revelation, I continued in a similar vein. "You see," I said, "there was one thing Tiff would never let me do." Ignoring the obvious reluctance of my listeners to hear another word, I finished with: "I finally got to taste roast suckling pig!"

Tiff had a somewhat self-contradictory policy on eating or refusing certain meats. Although he was a fervent fan of filet mignon — positively bloodthirsty — he never touched meat from the young or the small. No suckling pig, no lamb, no veal, no Cornish hens or guinea fowl or quail or squab. Certainly no rabbits. No wild animals: no venison or moose or bear.

Tiff's policy had consequences. It seemed every time we were invited to dinner at a private home in France, the main dish contained some form of what Tiff saw as Peter Rabbit. One prominent Ottawa restaurateur greeted us with an apology: "Oh, I'm so sorry, Tiff. Tonight, on the menu, we're featuring both Peter and Bambi!"

To be honest, I am now besotted with suckling pig. I enjoyed this loss of virginity almost as much as the first — when I was innocent and fourteen — and had this friend in high school.

During the years before the Cotignac property sold, I travelled back and forth a couple of times — using our Cotignac handyman, John Bertram, to get me to the Nice airport or to pick me up there. A pleasant gent from Stratford, John Pflance, did the same for me on the Canadian end.

One time, arriving in France, I remarked to John Bertram that his Canadian counterpart always provided cold bottled water and the day's newspaper for my trip. When it came time to fly back to Canada, I was both amused and delighted when John suddenly pulled off the Provençal superhighway into a rest stop, got out of the car, opened the trunk and brought to me — all beautifully packaged — a complete French breakfast: croissant, butter, jam, orange juice and a thermos of coffee. And — oh, yes — a copy of our local newspaper, *Le Var-Matin*. I thanked him profusely, and then suggested that he had given me an idea. I would use his kindness and generosity to set up a competition between the two drivers, to see how far they would go in trying to outdo each other.

I told him I had visions of a full-course hot meal and dancing boys.

I never saw the dancing boys, but did acquire something much, much better.

A companion.

IN 2003, A LITTLE OVER A year after Tiff died, I received a letter from a young man in Fort St. John, in the far north of British Columbia. His name was Trevor Greene, and he declared himself to be an ardent fan of the work of Timothy Findley. He was just completing high school, and was planning on being in Stratford that summer to take part in a Festival project designed to acquaint young people with theatre. Could we meet?

I was sorry to have to reply him that I would, in fact, be in France during the period of his stay. I wished him well with his Festival experience. To be frank, I forgot all about him.

That fall, when I was back in Stratford, I got a call from someone named Trevor Greene. I was at a loss, and admitted that although his name seemed familiar, I had no idea who he was. My memory was soon sorted out. It turned out that Trevor had remained in Ontario well beyond the time he had originally planned to return to the west.

Could we meet?

I decided to be polite and set up a time, offering to provide him a lunch.

I admitted a tall, good-looking young fellow into the apartment. He was well spoken and had a quick mind. I soon learned from him about his family background: both his parents had native blood — his father Cree and his mother Cowichan. Trevor, himself, wanted desperately to be an actor — and possibly also a writer. Hence his interest in Tiff.

I expressed interest, but I had met so many young people who wanted to be one or the other. I did, however, have one unexpressed reservation. Trevor had a facial tic, which he could mostly suppress for short periods, but with great difficulty. He identified the condition as "low level Tourette's syndrome."

Over the next two years, he made repeated visits to Stratford and we slowly became friends. Please note: there are no quotation marks around that last word. Friends. Yes, it turned out he's gay, but sex does not play a role in our friendship.

Then disaster; in 2004, Trevor developed one of the most

painful and difficult conditions I have ever witnessed, Dry Eye Syndrome. The afflicted person's tears dry up; not the tears that signal emotion, but the much more vital tears that lubricate the eyes. Without them, the patient is in constant and agonizing pain and suffers an almost-total inability to spend time in something vital to Trevor's happiness — reading.

Eventually, he moved in with me, and started struggling with the problems of finding treatment for his disease. There is one drug that's effective — Restasis — but it's available only for veterinary use in Canada. Trevor — one of the most enterprising people I've ever known — found an American friend willing to smuggle a small supply across the border. Then he learned of an experimental Restasis program in nearby Guelph, and managed to become enrolled in it. Almost a year later, he was free of the dreadful condition.

Now we have a superb friendship. We share the cooking; often I serve as *sous chef* to his remarkably rapid acquisition of culinary skills. He provides the energy — and the arms and legs — for all the running around for shopping and errands, as well as all the heavy lifting and the reaching for anything too high for me.

(Everything, that is, except the upper stretches of our living room walls, which I recently decided needed new colours. Trevor has never painted anything. Having decided he bloody well wasn't going to learn here, I managed to cling to a stepladder for weeks, getting the job done myself.)

Whenever he can find the time, he's busy with words: reading and writing.

It all works out very well and we have fun. Trevor has a very quick wit, I've discovered. As Tiff and I used to, we often indulge in the kind of banter that used to circulate around an Algonquin Hotel table in New York, where such wits as Dorothy Parker and Robert Benchley once gathered. There, if anyone happened to say something with an unintended double meaning (such as, in discussing the most comfortable position for falling asleep, "I do best on my back") there would be a chorus of "As the girl said to the sailor!" In British theatre — and, ultimately, in theatres here — that would become "As the actress said to the bishop."

Here's a recent example with us. I have two sets of bifocals — each with different lower halves. One set is for reading from the page — while another has a longer focal length for reading a computer screen. The problem is that I keep forgetting to change glasses when I finish a spell of work at the computer. Recently, when Trevor found me sitting on my sofa, trying to do a crossword puzzle with the wrong lenses, he repeated his usual response by silently exchanging glasses. I felt apologetic, and explained why I kept forgetting. "You see," I said. "The top half is the same."

To which he instantly replied, "As the transsexual said to the bishop."

It is not a pretty sight — an eighty-year-old, helplessly giggling.

BEFORE TREVOR CAME TO STAY, I took one quite unforgettable trip to Tokyo. When Tiff died, I inherited his air points — and, upon hearing that a theatre in Tokyo was about to mount a Japanese version of *Elizabeth Rex* in 2004, I invited the original production's director, Martha Henry, to accompany me across the Pacific to see it. Because of Tiff's air points, we were able to travel business class, which was glorious. All the way over,

Martha studied her lines for a one-woman play she was about to do in Montreal — *Rose* — the story of a Holocaust survivor.

We were met in Tokyo by a pleasant young couple who had come to meet us in Stratford when the Tokyo production was first planned. We all took a bus downtown, which took about the same amount of time it takes to get from Stratford to Pearson Airport — almost two hours. We were installed in a hotel high on a hill in the middle of the city, right beside a Shinto temple.

The next afternoon, we were taken to the theatre — which, to our amazement, was on the twentieth floor of a high-rise hotel. Martha, being Martha, had packed two huge paper sacks with gift-wrapped bits of Canadiana to give to the Japanese cast — tiny bottles of maple syrup, packets of maple sugar, etc. We took all this stuff to the theatre, where we learned that there would be a public dress rehearsal in the afternoon, followed by a quick supper with the show's bilingual director, and then the opening night performance.

We suggested that perhaps, before the public dress began, we could be taken around the dressing rooms to distribute Martha's gifts. In each room, we were greeted with utter puzzlement. The gifts were accepted, with many questioning glances shared among the occupants. We finally realized that the cast had no idea who we were or why we were there.

As we began to watch the afternoon performance, we felt just as lost as they had been. Much of the play's comedy occurs in the first act. The audience sat through the whole of it, silent and stony faced, while we — who couldn't understand a word of the dialogue, but who did know the text well — chortled away, utterly alone in our amusement.

Had the play's humour been lost in translation?

The curtain came down on the first act and there was total silence. Not a single pair of hands came together in applause.

At the intermission, all was explained. For an audience in Japan, if the play is considered to be one with a serious theme it is impolite to laugh, no matter how funny any given moment may be. And, just as our audiences do not applaud at the end of each movement in a symphony, Japanese audiences save their applause for the final curtain.

The applause this audience saved was thunderous.

The second time we were taken around the dressing rooms, the actors knew who we were and why we were there. There were hugs and kisses and tears all around!

That night, I met the Japanese translator of *The Wars*, with whom I'd had a long correspondence about some of the differences between our two languages. For example: he had asked about two of the characters who were described as brothers. Who was the elder and who the younger? This mattered, as there is no word in Japanese for "brother" — only for "elder brother" and "younger brother."

The production itself was admirable — particularly the casting and performance of Elizabeth. The actress was tall — for a Japanese woman — and magnificent. I called her "reverse Kabuki," because she often played male roles in Tokyo. Ned, on the other hand, was a bit of a disappointment. It turned out that he was not actually an actor, but a dancer who had suffered an injury that had ended his dancing career. He hadn't acted before — and, to tell the truth, that pretty well sums up his performance. Shakespeare, on the other hand, was played in an older, more stylized manner — which had the great value of setting him apart from everyone else on stage.

After the opening performance, we went out with the whole cast for dinner in the largest restaurant I have ever seen. I swear it covered a city block. It featured a range of Japanese dishes that was both greater and more delicious than any I had ever eaten.

Martha and I got to see Kabuki theatre, which was completely sold out; fortunately, however, our play's director was a friend of the star, and so we got tickets. The stage was vast; four Canadian proscenia could have fit into it. It seemed miles deep. The show was magnificent, as was the intermission. It included a full sit-down Japanese meal served in a beautiful bento box.

We asked to be taken to see Van Gogh's *Sunflowers*, which we understood was in a Tokyo gallery. Two things about it both amazed and amused us. Like the theatre, it was in a high-rise hotel, on the forty-fifth floor. As you left the elevator, you could see *Sunflowers* far away down the hall, flanked by another Van Gogh and a Gauguin. That was amazing. What was amusing was that both walls, all the way down the hall, were covered with works by — of all people — Grandma Moses!

Now my travels are accomplished in the highly pleasant and useful company of young Trevor. His energy and strength are invaluable, especially to someone in his eighties. We've driven coast-to-coast in Canada, but flown to Newfoundland. We've been to Venice twice, to France three times and to the Caribbean. And now, we're talking about where to go next year. It's a good thing that my own work — and Tiff's — have provided me with fairly generous retirement funds.

Still, I must realize that I am no longer young and old friends — sadly — are leaving, one by one.

The first to go was Bill Hutt.

I'm so glad that, before he went, I was able to confess something to him. It concerned one of his early Lears — in the sixties — for a Canadian Players tour. It was the infamous Eskimo Lear, designed by Herbert Whittaker and directed by David Gardner. It was set in an Eskimo kingdom, with a few overtones of Viking culture thrown in — the king wore a helmet with horns. The cast included Tobi Weinberg, a Regina actress who played the Madam in our production of *The Balcony* by Jean Genet, and my former companion Herb Foster as the Fool in a fool's cap, which made him look remarkably like an Arctic hare. My confession? Ever since I first saw the show at the Crest Theatre in Toronto, I have referred to is as "No, No, Nanook."

It was wonderful to hear Hutt laugh …

Although there have been many departures, I am still surrounded by friends. Martha Henry and her husband, Rod Beattie, go way back in my life. Sylvia Tyson remains one of my closest friends; she even lets Trevor and me use her New York apartment on occasion. Other theatre friends include the actor Patricia Collins and directors Marti Maraden and Diana Leblanc.

I still receive a lovely visit to Stratford each year from two of my oldest friends, John and Norma Moore, now in Montreal — my fellow members of Community Players in Saskatoon during my university days.

I remain in close contact with Mary Adachi — Tiff's copy editor on everything from *The Wars* on. I remember the horror with which the HarperCollins publisher, Iris Tupholme, received word that we sometimes called Mary "The Yellow Peril." Iris didn't want to believe it, but thought we might be referring disrespectfully to the fact that Mary is a Japanese Canadian. Not at all. It was simply because each time we went to Mary's house to go through the final version of a Findley book — after a lovely Japanese lunch — out would come the manuscript — bristling with hundreds of little markers, each indicating some quarrel Mary had with the wording. The markers, you see, were little strips made out of Post-it notes, coloured yellow.

I also regularly see Vincent Tovell, who produced many of the shows I wrote. He's almost ten years older than I am, but still vitally intelligent and in touch with every important issue of the day. His mother was a Massey, and whenever he and Tiff started reminiscing about that family, I would fall into a comfortable silence.

From the writing world I have two quite extraordinary friends, Margaret Atwood and Graeme Gibson. Graeme's novel *Perpetual Motion* remains one of my favourites, while his two collections — *The Book of Birds* and *The Book of Beasts* — are superb creations.

I have special memories of Peggy and her voice. Once, not too long ago, we were at lunch at the home of Jane and Tony Urquhart in Stratford. Also there were Alice Munro and her husband, Gerry, along with Peggy and Graeme. During dinner, the subject of unusual publishing venues came up, and Trevor asked Alice if she had ever been published in *Playboy* — a magazine that afforded him much pleasure for its fiction. Alice allowed that she had never appeared there, but Peggy piped up that she had. Alice inquired, "As the centrefold?"

What a glorious image that conjured up!

At the end of the meal, I heard Trevor apologizing to Peggy: "I'm sorry, Margaret — I think I interrupted you a couple of times this afternoon." Peggy fixed him with that lowered-glasses look of hers and intoned: "Trevor. Why are you apologizing to me? You interrupted everyone."

I will long treasure a moment when Peggy came up with the perfect squelch. It followed her talk in a Massey Lecture series on the subject of debt. A rather pompous young academic stood up with the question: "Miss Atwood, you have spoken much about debt, but I am wondering, what you, Margaret Atwood — personally — what would you do about debt?" Peggy lowered her head, directed her gaze over her glasses, leaned forward and said: "Give. This. Lecture."

Peggy's schedule of writing, travelling and speaking must be exhausting. I remember the time Trevor called her up and asked if she could give him a brief statement in support of Tiff's novel, *Not Wanted on the Voyage*, which had been chosen as one of the novels to be championed by various celebrities on the CBC's *Canada Reads*.

It was a tired Peggy who came to the phone to hear his request. Her tone was even flatter than usual when she asked, "Why does he want it?"

Trevor was puzzled, but replied, "Why does who want it?"

"Keanu Reeves."

"Keanu Reeves? Oh, no. Canada Reads."

Tired as she was, Peggy offered some excellent support for the book. It didn't win, but came in second — behind the work of an author Tiff had much admired and to whom, in that author's early days, he had offered much support — Paul Quarrington, now sadly gone from our midst.

THIS BRINGS UP A SUBJECT ABOUT which neither of us ever had a great deal to say, even though we regularly became involved with it. I'm referring to a practice which, in the eyes of many — including Tiff and me — is an obligation: senior members of a group offering support and assistance to worthy juniors as they progress. I simply can't remember everyone who succeeded in attracting Tiff's attention, although I do recall that the group included Marnie Woodrow and Karen Connelly.

The assistance can take many forms: for writers, perhaps a laudatory endorsement to be used on the jacket of a new book. What Margaret Laurence used to call "a tender message," and she sent many of them, as did Tiff.

It could also be avowed support for a grant application — or enthusiasm expressed to a publisher or agent about the work of an as-yet-unknown writer. Tiff certainly supported many grant applications, but had less success with publishers. Of all the manuscripts he asked publishers to consider, only one was ever accepted — and then, ironically, not until one publisher's young editor moved to another house and eventually achieved the power to publish the piece in question.

I occasionally worked with apprentice documentary writers, although not always with success. Having been impressed with one young writer's unfilmed script, I managed to persuade a CBC producer to engage the chap to create the narration for a show I had originally been hired to work on. The deal was this: if, for any reason, the newcomer was unable to come up with a fully acceptable script, I would take over completely — for the same low price that was deemed suitable for a neophyte.

By the time the film was ready to receive its narration script, my young protégé was off in some remote part of the world, working on another project. I took over, happily and without resentment; I liked the show.

Under certain circumstances, our support took the form of an outright gift of money. I see no need to mention names or amounts — indeed, I see every reason not to — but I can give you an explanation for why we did it.

Tiff and I were both great fans of the American writer Thornton Wilder. My undergradute days brought me to read and love his novels. For Tiff, it was working in a British production of a Wilder play, *The Matchmaker*, that brought the two together. Tiff earned the privilege of having Wilder as an early mentor.

In *The Matchmaker* the heroine, Dolly Levi, expresses a principle that caught us both: "Money is like manure — it's not worth a thing unless it's spread around, helping young things to grow!"

Words to live by.

Occasionally there were other ways to help. Both with Stone Orchard and at the Stratford condo, whenever extended absences were necessary, the space might be offered to a young writer seeking a rent-free retreat in order to finish a piece of work. Whenever Trevor and I are away for a while, the process still continues.

None of this is bragging. The process, whatever form it takes, simply remains something both proper and practical. Sometimes, I think, Tiff and I also saw it as a means of repaying help we each received when we needed it.

WHAT HAS KEPT ME GOING — APART from the wonder of old friends — can be summed up in two words that begin with a T: Trevor and travel. And now, of course, they happen together.

On one of our New York visits, I was a bit nervous about

being on the streets on a certain night, but Trevor had booked us into the theatre. So off we went. It was a glorious evening. The play was a wonderful production of the award-winning *August: Osage County*. We left the theatre and headed for Times Square, through which we had to pass in order to catch the 42nd Street bus that would take us home. The square was absolutely packed with people. Just as we entered it, all hell broke loose.

I've never been in such an exuberant, noisy or massive crowd. A roaring surge of people started to pull me away from Trevor. I saved myself by grabbing onto his backpack — and we finally made it to safety.

Just as we had entered Times Square, the huge CNN screen there announced: "OBAMA WINS!" Unforgettable.

There have been other wonderful moments in my travels with Trevor, some of them quieter.

On our last visit to Venice, we were on one of the vaporettos that run up and down the Grand Canal. Trevor was carrying a book, as he always does. One of our fellow passengers, a British woman, noticing that he was reading the work of a British author, and having misinterpreted our North American accents as American, made a friendly observation: "You must think our spelling eccentric, which of course is how we view yours." Trevor explained that we were Canadian, whereupon the poor woman — mortified to think that she had grossly insulted us in thinking that we were Americans — launched into endless and somewhat embarrassing apologies. All the while we were surrounded by American tourists, who, if they noticed our conversation at all, simply stared at us and then resumed staring at whatever we were passing.

I AM NOW MAKING ALL KINDS of discoveries of what it is like to be old. One day, a few months before Trevor moved in, I discovered that I am a walking anachronism. There was a young man I had met a few years earlier. He was a friend of a friend of a friend; very pleasant company, and extremely good-looking. One day, when he was visiting Stratford, he asked if I had any photos of Stone Orchard or the house in Cotignac, both of which he'd heard about from our mutual acquaintances. As it happened, I did. On book tours, so many people asked to see shots of both places that Tiff and I had made up little albums. I hauled them out and we sat on the living room sofa to look at them. After a while (how to say this?) we weren't looking at photographs any longer. A few moments later, it seemed appropriate — if not obligatory — that I reach down and do a little fondling. Suddenly, my fingers detected some sort of ecstatic shiver through the fabric of his trousers.

"Good grief!" I said. "How did you do that?"

His answer left me speechless.

"Actually, Bill, what you've been holding onto is the cell phone in my pocket — and I just got a call."

ONE THING THAT HASN'T CHANGED IN my life as I grow older is my proclivity to fall into verbal traps.

Towards the end of Tiff's life, we transferred ownership of our theatre memorabilia to the University of Guelph: set and costume designs, production photos and props from plays Tiff had written or in which either of us had appeared. We gave up ownership, but not possession. The university kindly allowed us to keep all the material.

Not long ago, I was shipping other archival material out

to the University of Calgary. Somehow the question of what I was keeping came up as I talked to the courier clerk. I tried to explain the difference between ownership and possession. "You see," I said, "Guelph now owns all our theatre stuff, but I still have it. I still possess it." And then, intending to say that, otherwise, my walls would be bare, out came: "Otherwise, my balls would beware!" Reverend Spooner strikes again!

Embarrassment led to silence, which quickly turned into departure.

I keep thinking of something Tiff once said to me. *Bouillon de culture* attempted on several occasions to book Tiff for an interview; this television show was hosted by Bernard Pivot, who always ended his interviews with the same set of questions. The final question was always: "When you reach the pearly gates, what would you like to hear said to you?"

Tiff told me how he was prepared to reply.

"You're late!"

Tiff is still with me. Memories. Yearnings. Thoughts.

The last interview he actually did was with the wonderful Eleanor Wachtel. At the end, she asked him: "So, Tiff — what's next?" His instant reply was: "Death." Then, he roared with laughter and said: "BUT!" and began to sing that song from *Annie*, "Tomorrow." The last thing to be heard in that interview is that glorious, husky Findley laugh.

Will there be sun for me tomorrow?

I hope so. I've had the most wonderful life. Glorious people, fabulous places and more love and laughter than can be imagined. It's hard to express how grateful I am for my life: grateful for everything, but not grateful to anything. I've never felt the need to imagine some all-powerful being who is responsible for creating everything I know and love. Many have been imagined. I view the various divinities that are worshipped in different ways by different groups, the various eternal paradises that are promised, as wishful thinking. I hope that all such worshippers will allow me to find my own way out of this life, in much the same way I found my way into it: innocent of knowledge about how, where, when and why everything I know came into being.

Or — is there some incomprehensible eternity that has no beginnings and no endings? I don't know. I do know that I want to hold onto *my* sense of gratitude — for the loves I've shared — particularly Tiff's, and Trevor's — for the places I've visited — and for all the words — all those magical words with which I've worked and played.

What will my experience of death be like? By then, will I still have words to express what I feel?

Now, as my life begins to come full circle, I think of my very earliest memory — of falling asleep in my crib, when there was only one time: now. And nothing I knew had a name.

I remember the utter comfort of sinking into that nightly nothingness I would come to call "sleep." The realm without images — the place that produced no memories.

Now, with a lifetime of images and memories, I could live without words.

And, if need be, I could die without them, too.

Complete.

And contented.